CULTURES OF THE WORLD

Grenada

Guek-Cheng Pang

mc **Marshall Cavendish**
Benchmark
New York

PICTURE CREDITS

Cover: © Buddy Mays / Alamy

19th era 2/Alamy: 31 • Armand-Photo-Travel/Alamy: 118 • Audrius Tomonis: 135 • Axion Photographic Agency: 109 • Besstock: 43 • Charles Stirling (Travel)/Alamy: 98, 100 • Cotton Coulson/National Geographic/ Getty Images: 38 • David G. Houser: 12, 13, 17, 18, 37, 47, 50, 77, 89, 92, 120 • Eye Ubiquitous / Alamy: 26 • Eye Ubiquitous/Alamy: 119 • Fox Photos/Getty Images: 30 • Grenada Board of Tourism: 104 • Holger Leue/ Lonely Planet Images: 66, 97 • Hulton Archive/Getty Images: 29 • Hutchison Library: 71, 80, 83, 112, 115 • Jan Butchofsky/Dave G. Houser: 25, 68, 85, 86 • Jewel Samad/AFP/Getty Images: 101 • Margie Politzer/Lonely Planet Images: 5 • Nik wheeler/Alamy: 88 • North Wind Picture Archives: 21, 22, 23, 27, 69 • Photolibrary: 3, 6, 7, 8, 9, 10, 11, 14, 15, 20, 32, 42, 48, 52, 53, 54, 56, 57, 60, 61, 62, 64, 65, 74, 75, 78, 79, 84, 87, 90, 91, 95, 96, 102, 105, 110, 114, 116, 117, 122, 123, 124, 126, 127, 130, 131 • Richard I'Anson/Lonely Planet Images: 1, 59, 94, 106, 111 • Sigrid Estrada/Liaison/Getty Images: 103 • Steven L. Raymer/National Geographic/Getty Images: 28 • Topham Picturepoint: 16, 24, 33, 34, 36, 39, 41, 45, 46, 67, 107, 108 • Trip Photolibrary: 49, 51, 72 • World Pictures/Alamy: 128

PRECEDING PAGE

A young Grenadian girl in Gouyave village.

Publisher (U.S.): Michelle Bisson
Editors: Deborah Grahame-Smith, Stephanie Pee
Copyreader: Sherry Chiger
Designers: Nancy Sabato, Bernard Go
Cover picture researcher: Connie Gardner
Picture researchers: Thomas Khoo, Joshua Ang

Marshall Cavendish Benchmark
99 White Plains Road
Tarrytown, NY 10591
Website: www.marshallcavendish.us

© Times Media Private Limited 1999
© Marshall Cavendish International (Asia) Private Limited 2011
® "Cultures of the World" is a registered trademark of Times Publishing Limited.

Originated and designed by Times Media Private Limited
An imprint of Marshall Cavendish International (Asia) Private Limited
A member of Times Publishing Limited

Marshall Cavendish is a trademark of Times Publishing Limited.

All Internet sites were correct and accurate at the time of printing. All monetary figures in this publication are in U.S. dollars.

Library of Congress Cataloging-in-Publication Data
Pang, Guek-Cheng, 1950-
  Grenada / Guek-Cheng Pang. -- 2nd ed.
    p. cm. — (Cultures of the world)
  Summary: "Provides comprehensive information on the geography, history, wildlife, governmental structure, economy, cultural diversity, peoples, religion, and culture of Grenada"—Provided by publisher.
  Includes bibliographical references and index.
  ISBN 978-1-60870-216-9
  1. Grenada—Juvenile literature. I. Title.
  F2056.C45 2011
  972.9845--dc22   2010019807

Printed in China
7 6 5 4 3 2 1

CONTENTS

INTRODUCTION

GRENADA: IS IT IN SPAIN? IS THIS THE PLACE THE AMERICANS invaded? These are two responses one gets when the subject of Grenada arises. Many people do not know anything about this beautiful island in the Caribbean, which explains why it remains relatively unspoiled even today.

But to learn about Grenada is to discover a place of great natural beauty, with verdant volcanic hillsides ringed by miles of spotless white- and black-sand beaches. Grenada was shaped by a complex history and was often a pawn in the wars of other nations. The country experienced the hardships of slavery and survived the mass migrations of its people. A quiet place, it was relatively unknown until a revolution in 1983 caused it to be the only Caribbean nation to be invaded by the United States.

Cultures of the World: Grenada also discovers a people who are proud to be black, proud to be Caribbean, and most of all, proud to be Grenadian.

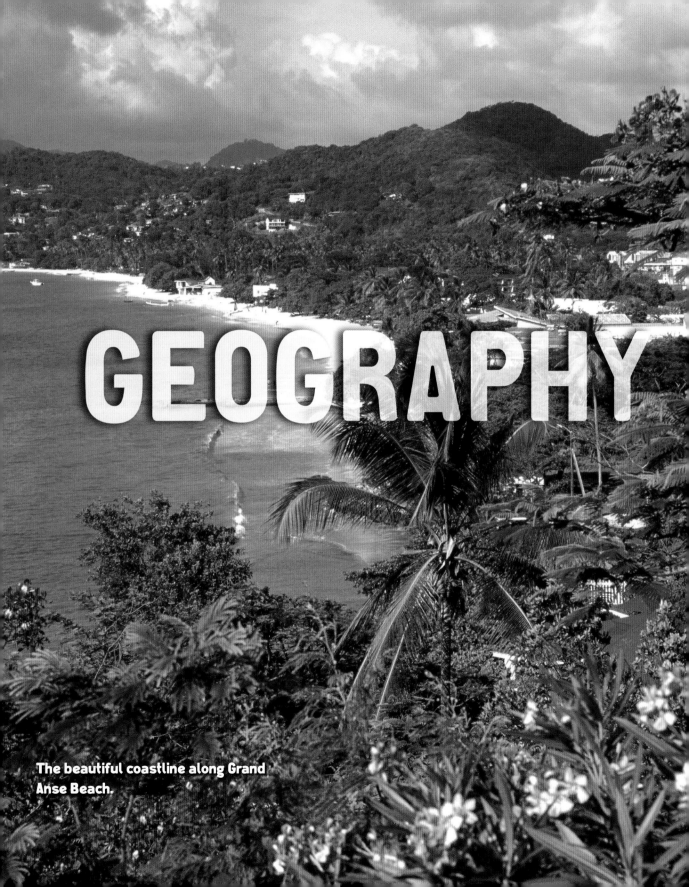

GEOGRAPHY

The beautiful coastline along Grand Anse Beach.

GRENADA IS AN ISLAND NATION in the Caribbean Sea. It is part of an archipelago of more than 7,000 islands, many of them nothing more than little rocky outcrops poking above the surface of the ocean.

The nation of Grenada consists of the island of Grenada itself, which is about 21 miles (34 km) long and 12 miles (19 km) wide at its widest, and the smaller islands of Carriacou and Petite Martinique plus more than 20 very small islands and cays. Carriacou lies 23 miles (37 km) northeast

Clear skies and calm waters off Paradise Beach at L'Esterre Bay.

The nation of Grenada is made up of three main islands: Grenada, Carriacou, and Petite Martinque. Grenada is part of the Caribbean islands, and it is speculated that these islands used to link Florida to Venezuela. Grenada enjoys a warm climate all year round but is subjected to hurricanes, which can be very destructive. The wettest months are from June to December.

of Grenada Island. Petite Martinique is another 2.5 miles (4 km) northeast of Carriacou. The three main islands have a total landmass of 133 square miles (344 square km). The island of Grenada is 120 square miles (311 square km), about twice the size of Washington, D.C., while Carriacou is 13 square miles (34 square km), and Petite Martinique is 486 acres (197 ha).

THE CARIBBEAN ISLANDS

The Caribbean islands lie south of Florida, separating the Caribbean Sea to the west from the Atlantic Ocean to the east. The largest islands in the group — Cuba, Jamaica, Hispaniola, and Puerto Rico—make up the Greater Antilles. North of these four large islands is the Bahamas.

The islands of the Lesser Antilles lie to the east and south of Puerto Rico. The Lesser Antilles are divided into two groups: the Leeward Islands and the Windward Islands. The Windward Islands are Dominica, Martinique,

An aerial view of the Grenadines, which form part of the Caribbean islands.

Saint Lucia, Saint Vincent, Barbados, the Grenadines, and Grenada and its adjacent islands, while the Leeward Islands include those between Anguilla and Guadeloupe and their adjacent islands. Finally there is a group of islands closest to the Venezuelan coast: Trinidad and Tobago, Aruba, Bonaire, and Curaçao.

Geologists believe that during the last ice age, all the Caribbean islands formed a land bridge that linked Florida with Venezuela. But this landmass was submerged by the sea in a series of earthquakes and volcanic eruptions so that only the tops of the mountains remain above water, as islands.

BALMY ALL YEAR

Lying south of the Tropic of Cancer, Grenada has a warm climate year-round. The average daily temperature is 81°F (27°C), and this does not vary much throughout the year. The coolest months are from December to March, and the hottest from August to November. There is a greater difference in temperature during the day, as daytime temperatures can hit above 86°F

The parish of Saint George enjoys a warm climate all year.

The most destructive hurricane in the island's recorded history was Hurricane Ivan, which hit Grenada on September 7, 2004, and damaged or destroyed 90 percent of the island's homes.

(30°C), falling to the low 70s°F (low 20s°C) at night. Although the Caribbean islands are in the hurricane belt, Grenada is less affected than other islands by these destructive winds. Many heavy thunderstorms pass over Grenada during the hurricane season.

RAINFALL

Instead of summer and winter, Grenada has wet and dry seasons. The dry season is from January to May, when the hills turn brown due to lack of rain and rivers are low. The heaviest rainfall occurs from June to December, making the land green once again.

The highest rainfall occurs in the central mountains and in the sheltered valleys on the windward side of the mountains. These receive an average of 160 inches (406 cm) a year. The coastal regions are drier, getting about 50 inches (127 cm) a year, especially on the leeward side of the island. The southern tip is the driest part of the island. Grenada also receives convectional rain. This occurs when the land heats up during the day. This heats the air, which rises and creates a powerful updraft. As the air rises, it cools, and the moisture it contains is released as rain that often falls in the mid-afternoon.

Rain in the main street of Hillsborough.

TOPOGRAPHY

Like the other Windward Islands, Grenada has a rich and varied terrain. There are high mountains, rain forests, deep river valleys, beautiful lakes,

HURRICANES

Hurricanes are a significant climatic phenomenon in the Caribbean. In the summer, strong winds develop in troughs of low pressure in the eastern Caribbean, bringing unsettled, overcast weather, often accompanied by heavy rains. Sometimes these winds gather enough force to become a hurricane. "Hurricane" comes from a Carib word, huracan (HU-rah-cahn). It refers to a tropical storm with heavy rain and winds that exceed 74 mph (119 km/h). These high-velocity winds blow in a counterclockwise direction around a low-pressure center, known as the eye of the storm, where the winds are calm. Yet the strongest winds rage most fiercely at the points closest to the eye. As the hurricane roars through, the area affected by the storm may be more than 150 miles (241 km) wide. The hurricane season is from June to November, with the most frequent occurrences in August and September. On average, about five to eight hurricanes develop a year, but many fizzle out before they reach land.

The impressive Concord Falls plunges 33 feet (10 m) into a pool.

some desertlike areas, strings of beautiful white- and black-sand beaches, and deep and sheltered harbors.

The highest peak is Mount Saint Catherine, which is 2,757 feet (840 m) high. Other mountains on the island—Mount Granby, Mount Lebanon, and Mount Sinai—rise more than 2,000 feet (610 m) above sea level. A number of rivers begin in the central mountains and flow to the sea.

Grenadians may call the same river by many names, depending on which part of the country or which village it passes through. Major rivers include the Great River, which flows through the parish of Saint Andrew, Saint John's River, and Saint Patrick's River.

LAKES AND BEACHES

There is much evidence on Grenada Island, especially on the north coast, of previous volcanic activity: volcanic vents, black-sand beaches, and sulfurous springs. Several extinct volcanic craters are now filled with beautiful lakes,

According to experts Lake Antoine is the perfect example of a crater lake.

such as Levera Pond and Lake Antoine in the northeast, and Grand Etang Lake in the center of the island.

Grand Etang Lake is 1,700 feet (518 m) above sea level. The area around it is a national park and a forest reserve. The park can easily be reached by road and by paths that allow visitors to enjoy the thick natural rain forest that surrounds the crater. Lake Antoine is just 20 feet (6 m) above sea level, and it is 16 acres (6 ha) in size. It was formed 12,000 to 15,000 years ago during Grenada's final stage of volcanic activity.

The Grenadian coastline, which stretches for more than 80 miles (129 km), is indented by many beautiful bays and lovely beaches. The two most spectacular beaches are on the southern tip of the island: Lance aux Epines and the Grand Anse.

RAIN FORESTS

There is a wide variety of natural vegetation on Grenada Island: lush tropical rain forests, woodlands, mangrove swamps, and desert scrubland. Tropical

The lush tropical rain forests of Grenada.

rain forests flourish on the windward side of the mountains. Trees that grow more than 100 feet (30.5 m) tall are covered with mosses and ferns. Seasonal rain forests grow in slightly drier areas. They originally covered most of the lowland regions and can still be found on the leeward side of the island. Dry forests grow in regions that receive between 30 and 50 inches (76 and 127 cm) of rain a year. Trees that grow here are rarely more than 30 feet (9 m) tall, and they lose their leaves in the dry season. Where people have cleared the forests, they have left flat, dry savannas with scrub trees. Thorny trees and cacti grow on the dry leeward coasts. Mangrove swamps, trees, and shrubs that can survive in shallow and muddy saltwater cover some coastal areas.

FLORA

The tropical climate supports a vast number of economically useful trees. Fruit trees such as mango, papaya, and soursop are grown everywhere.

The bougainvillea is Grenada's national flower.

There are palm trees of many kinds—date palms, queen palms, royal palms, and coconut palms. The coconut palm is extremely useful; it provides food, drink, oil for cooking, and building materials. Other common trees are the banyan, the mahogany, and the calabash. Banyans are large trees with spreading branches and roots that hang from the branches to the ground. The mahogany, a native of the Caribbean, is valued for its wood. Calabash trees have large round fruit with hard shells that can be hollowed out and made into bowls, utensils, and craft objects. Beautiful flowering plants, including orchids, gingers, hyacinths, bougainvilleas, hibiscuses, allamandas, frangipani, and oleanders, are found everywhere. The bougainvillea is Grenada's national flower.

FAUNA

When the Europeans arrived in the 15th century, they discovered limited animal life because few animals had been able to cross the water from South

The mongoose preys on fish, chickens, crabs, and other small island animals.

America. They did find bats and rodents, including hutias, large and tasty animals that reminded the Spanish of rabbits. The mongoose is commonly found in Grenada. It was brought by sugarcane farmers to help get rid of the cane rat. But the mongoose, being a daytime hunter, was not much help in killing the nocturnal rat. Instead it became a nuisance, preying on other small island animals.

There are several varieties of reptiles, including caimans, snakes, and lizards. Iguanas, which can grow to 5 feet (1.5 m) or more in length, are hunted by some who consider them a delicacy. But the iguana has fallen prey to the mongoose. There are no poisonous snakes or insects on the island. Troops of mona monkeys, introduced from West Africa centuries ago, live in the forested areas.

There are many kinds of birds, butterflies, and insects. The Grenada dove is Grenada's national bird. It lives only in Grenada and is severely endangered. There are probably fewer than 200 birds left on the island. Birds commonly found in Grenada include bananaquits, hummingbirds, swifts, wrens, flycatchers, thrushes, finches, and blackbirds. The island is a welcome stop for thousands of other birds on their migratory route from the north.

The seas are rich in marine life. The tropical fish are plentiful and colorful. There are groupers, snappers, angelfish, parrot fish, wrasses, and other reef inhabitants. Sea turtles come ashore from March to August to lay their eggs. There are several species: green turtles, leatherbacks, loggerheads, olive ridleys, and hawksbills. Turtles are sometimes sold in the fish markets because some people love to eat turtle meat. But hunting laws protect them during certain times of the year.

The buildings that dot the Carenage are an architectural blend of French colonial, English Georgian, and Victorian.

FRENCH-BUILT TOWNS

The capital of Grenada is Saint George's. About 33,700 people live and work in this town, which is on the south end of the island on a peninsula about a mile (1.6 km) long. Saint George's almost landlocked harbor, which is the crater of an extinct volcano, is so sheltered and deep that huge ocean liners are able to dock there.

The waterfront, known as the Carenage, has pink, ocher, and brick-red commercial buildings and warehouses, many dating from the 18th century. The town was designed by a former French governor, De Bellair de Saint-Aignan, in 1705, and planning was continued by the British when they took control of the island. A ridge divides Saint George's into two parts that are joined by the Sendall Tunnel, a 10-foot-wide (3-m-wide) tunnel constructed in 1894.

Grenville, an agricultural town, is the second largest city in Grenada and the main port on the east coast. It is a regional center for collecting cocoa, nutmeg, and other agricultural products. It was established in 1763 by the French, who called it La Baye. Victoria Street, the main street facing the waterfront, is the focus of the town's activity.

Carriacou's main town, Hillsborough, has government offices, a church, a marketplace, and shops.

Gouyave is the main town of Saint John Parish. Many of the residents here make their living from fishing. It is surrounded by nutmeg estates. The nutmeg processing station is the town's largest building.

GRENADA'S SISTER ISLANDS

Both Carriacou and Petite Martinique are part of the Grenadines, a chain of smaller islands that form a link between the larger island of Grenada in the south and Saint Vincent in the north. Carriacou and Petite Martinique are administered by Grenada, while most of the other Grenadines are run by Saint Vincent. The administrative line is so arbitrary that if one were to stand on the northern tip of Carriacou, at Rapid Point, one would actually be standing on Saint Vincent territory. There are no rivers on Carriacou or Petite Martinique. The residents have to collect rainwater in cisterns during the rainy season of June to December.

CARRIACOU The island of Carriacou, a name taken from a Carib word meaning "land of reefs," has a population of about 6,000. Like Grenada

Grenada has a few pristine natural areas that have been preserved. The Levera National Park on the northeast coast has dry woodland vegetation and a saltwater lagoon with a white-sand beach. The lagoon is sheltered by coral reefs with mangrove swamps on either side. La Sagesse Nature Center along the southeast coast has mangroves, coral reefs, and dry woodlands.

The largest national park on Grenada is the Grand Etang National Park, which covers the most mountainous central region of the island. Mount Saint Catherine, Grenada's highest mountain; Mount Qua Qua; and Mount Fedon are the jewels of the park. Crater Lake, which is in the crater of an extinct volcano, is a 13-acre (5-ha) expanse of cobalt-blue water. Visitors can hike in the park, using the many nature trails that have been developed.

Island, it has a central mountainous region that slopes down to the coasts. But like Petite Martinique, it has a drier climate, with an average annual rainfall of about 45 inches (114 cm). The earliest European settlers on the island were the French, who cleared the land and planted crops. Later the inhabitants of the island of Guadeloupe in the north arrived. When the British took control of the island in the 18th century, they grew cotton, sugarcane, coffee, cocoa, and indigo. The town of Windward is known for the shipwrights who came from Glasgow to build ships for the planters to transport the island's produce. Their descendants, bearing such Scottish names as McDonald, McLaren, MacFarland, and McLaurence, continue the tradition of building fishing boats and schooners today. Many families on Carriacou can also trace their ancestry to Africa and have retained many of their African traditions.

PETITE MARTINIQUE The much smaller island of Petite Martinique, where about 500 people live, is one of many volcanic cones forming islands in the Caribbean. The island was settled by French fishermen who built their own boats for fishing. Most of the men on the island today are fishermen, while some work on regional ships. Grenada has other smaller island dependencies in the Grenadine Islands that lie between the island of Grenada and Carriacou, such as Ile de Ronde, Kick-'em-Jenny, Green Bird, and Conference.

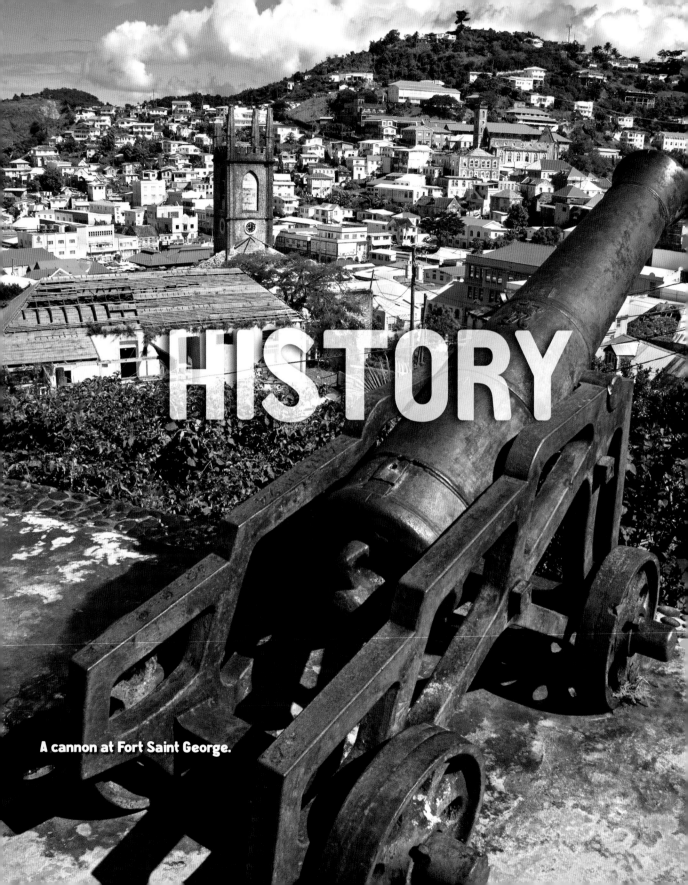

HISTORY

A cannon at Fort Saint George.

›T HE CARIBBEAN WAS INHABITED BY several groups of people long before Christopher Columbus arrived in the area in 1492. The earliest people, called Amerindians, came from the mainland of South America.

There were three groups of Amerindians. The first were the little-known Ciboneys. Their name, meaning "stone people," was given to them by the next group of people who arrived, the Arawaks. A peaceful people with an advanced civilization, the Arawaks lived on fish and cassava. Their petroglyphs can be seen in northern Grenada. A fierce and war-

A representation of the earliest Amerindians. They covered their heads, necks, arms, private parts, and feet with feathers, and the men had precious stones on their faces.

like race of Amerindians arrived next. They raided Arawak villages, killed the men, and enslaved the women. When the Europeans arrived there, they called these people Caribs, and the area came to be known as the Caribees. From this comes the name Caribbean.

GRENADA ON THE MAP

The Caribbean was first placed on the map in 1492 when in the employ of the Spanish, the Italian adventurer Christopher Columbus chanced on the Bahamas, landing on what is now called San Salvador. Columbus was searching for a westward passage to the East Indies. He explored the Bahamas and the

Christopher Columbus returning to Spain to report his great discovery to Queen Isabella.

north coast of Cuba before reaching the northeastern tip of another large island that he named Isla Española, known today as Hispaniola. Leaving some men behind to establish a small settlement, Columbus returned to Spain to report his discovery.

In 1498, on his third trip to the Caribbean, Columbus arrived at the north of Grenada, then called Camerhogne by the Amerindians. He named the island Concepción. The name was changed to Granada on the 16th century maps because the green hills reminded the Spanish sailors of Granada in Spain. The French, who settled on the island in the 1600s, changed the name to Grenade. When the British took possession of the island in 1763, the island came to be known as Grenada.

GOLD LURES EUROPEANS

Columbus's exciting discovery opened the floodgates of European exploitation. During the next few centuries the Caribbean islands were

The British *Vanguard* attacking Spanish ships in an attempt to capture their goods.

pawns in a game of power among the Spanish, the French, the British, and the Dutch.

Spain's interest was centered primarily on the islands of Cuba, Jamaica, and Puerto Rico, as gold could be found on them. Natives were forced to work in the gold mines until the gold was exhausted. The Arawak population was decimated, while the Caribs survived by retreating to the mountainous interiors and fighting back with some success.

When more gold was discovered in Peru and Mexico, the islands lost their importance. Nonetheless, Spanish ships were attacked by English and French pirates. The Dutch entered the fray later. They wanted the high-grade salt of Venezuela and tobacco, which was becoming popular in Europe.

The peace enjoyed during the 80 years following the Treaty of Utrecht allowed the economy of the region, which was largely dependent on the sugar industry, to grow rapidly.

After years of plundering Spanish possessions, the northern Europeans established their colonies in the Caribbean in the 1600s. Possession of the islands changed hands according to the fortunes of war in Europe.

EARLY COLONIZATION

The first colonies were run by merchants authorized by their governments to represent them. When the islands became economic burdens, the French government sold them to the merchant governors.

The Caribs resisted early colonization attempts by the Europeans. In 1650 two Frenchmen bought Saint Lucia, Grenade, and the Grenadines. Hostilities soon broke out. Three years later the French governor of Guadeloupe sent a force to Grenade that overran and killed the Caribs, finally cornering the last few in the north of the island. Rather than surrender, the remaining 40 Carib men, women, and children leaped off a cliff to their deaths. The cliff is now called Leapers' Bluff.

The River Antoine Rum Distillery was built in 1763. It houses one of the last remaining water-driven cane-crushers. During its peak Grenada was England's fourth-largest producer of sugar.

The island continued to change hands during the next two decades. After the Treaty of Utrecht in 1713 that ended the War of the Spanish Succession, the Caribbean enjoyed almost 80 years of peace and prosperity.

BRITAIN WINS GRENADA

In 1762 the British fleet sailed for Grenade and took it easily without even firing one shot. They promptly renamed the island Grenada. This victory was formalized in 1763 by the Treaty of Paris. This treaty also gave Britain control over Saint Vincent, Dominica, and Tobago.

Thousands of adventurers from the British Isles immediately sailed for the Caribbean. They cleared the forests, planted cane, built sugar mills, and imported thousands of slaves from Africa.

The new sugar plantations thrived on Saint Vincent and Grenada until 1795, when they were devastated by slave rebellions. In 1779, when the British fleet left the Caribbean to accompany some merchant ships to Britain, the French captured Saint Vincent. They sailed for Grenada and repossessed it after a two-day battle. But under the Treaties of Versailles signed in 1783, Grenada once again returned to British hands.

A bell hanging from a tree in Belmont Estate Plantation. This was once used to call slaves.

SLAVES AND REVOLTS

During the French occupation, the British settlers were treated badly. So when the British regained control, the French suffered before eventually rebelling in 1795. Led by Julien Fedon, a Grenadian planter of African and

French ancestry, thousands of slaves and "free colored" had the British on the run for more than a year.

Simultaneous slave revolts on multiple islands made it difficult for the British to rule in the Caribbean. Britain sent 17,000 troops to the Windward Islands in 1796 and ultimately did retake the islands, but only after meeting with fierce resistance.

Meanwhile the number of slaves in proportion to Europeans was rising. The white population decreased because there was no work for wage laborers. White settlers preferred to emigrate to North America in search of jobs. The planters became increasingly dependent on their slaves, training them to be house servants, drivers, and even bookkeepers and managers of their estates.

THE ROAD TO FREEDOM

Until the late 1700s, European governments and statesmen believed that slavery was necessary if they were to benefit from valuable exports such as sugar and other tropical products. But the political thinking was slowly changing.

Many began to realize that slavery was wrong. Emancipation in Grenada was gained with great difficulty, and more than 25 years passed between the end of the slave trade in the British Empire in 1807 and the abolition of slavery in 1834.

The increasing number of slave rebellions after 1815 strongly influenced public opinion in Britain. The Slavery Abolition Act was passed in August 1833, ordering the end of slavery in 1834. Emancipation took a longer time to take effect because the slaves were forced into a period of apprenticeship. It was only on August 1, 1838, at midnight, that the 750,000 slaves in the British

Slaves on the slave ship *Wildfire*, which was on its way to the United States.

colonies became free. There were celebrations, parades, and thanksgivings in the churches. For most slaves, freedom meant the right to live as self-reliant small farmers.

EMANCIPATION

Emancipation brought with it social and political difficulties. It increased the planters' costs at a time when sugar prices were falling. World production of sugar had increased dramatically, and the Caribbean islands had to compete with other sugar-producing regions. Beet sugar was also a cheap substitute for cane sugar.

The freed slaves were no longer willing to work in the sugar fields. They had each been given a small plot of land to grow their food and sell whatever surplus they might have. Most of them became independent farmers. When

Many freed slaves became independent farmers.

SLAVE TRADE

The coastal exploration of Africa and the invasion of the Americas by the Europeans in the 15th century gave rise to the slave trade. Portugal was the first European nation to begin importing slaves. The slaves were captured by other Africans and brought to trading posts and forts on the African coast before being sent on to Portugal to meet labor needs. Spain soon followed when the native populations of Latin America, who were forced to work on the plantations, could not survive the hard labor and exposure to European diseases. England entered the slave trade in the second half of the 16th century, fighting with Portugal to supply the Spanish colonies with slaves. In 1713 the British South Sea Company was given exclusive right to supply the Spanish colonies with slaves. Other countries—France, Holland, and Denmark as well as the American colonies—soon entered this lucrative business.

In 1792 Denmark became the first European country to abolish the slave trade, followed by Britain in 1807. In 1814, at the Congress of Vienna, Britain convinced nearly all the other foreign powers to adopt a similar policy, and finally all European states passed laws to prohibit the slave trade. In 1842 Britain and the United States signed the Webster-Ashburton Treaty in which both countries agreed to maintain a squadron on the African coast to enforce the prohibition of the trade.

Workers harvesting cocoa.

they did work on the estates, they were no longer submissive or willing to be cheap labor. The production of sugar for export stopped on the islands of Grenada, Saint Vincent, Dominica, Tobago, and Montserrat.

By 1856 most of the sugar estates in Grenada had been abandoned, and attention was switched to the planting of cocoa trees. New immigrants from Africa, India, and China arrived to fill the gaps left by the freed slaves. In 1846 and 1847, Portuguese workers arrived from the island of Madeira. But after 1850, most of the immigrants were indentured laborers from India, who came to work on the farms. Between 1838 and 1917, thousands of East Indian laborers arrived in Grenada.

FREEDOM TO VOTE

By 1763 Grenada had a system of representative government, in which a governor ruled with the help of a council that had limited powers. An elected assembly of officials made local laws.

An early cocoa mill. After emancipation there was little incentive to work for the country's economic growth, and the economy stagnated as a result.

Emancipation meant that the former slaves were now free British citizens with a right to vote if they had the same qualifications as the whites. Voters often had only to own a small amount of property to qualify. This allowed many blacks to vote in legislative elections. In 1877, however, Britain made Grenada a crown colony, and the elected House of Assembly was replaced by the government in London. This was done so that the British population would not be ruled by the black majority. Although the unrepresentative government slowed Grenada's route to self-government, it nevertheless was competent in maintaining public order and providing public services. There was little incentive to work for economic growth, though, so the island's economy stagnated.

In 1886 the colonial office in Britain united the islands of Grenada, Saint Vincent, Saint Lucia, and Tobago under the rule of one governor. Each island, however, had its own legislative council, police, judiciary, treasury, and public services. It wasn't until in 1974 that Grenada finally gained independence.

GOVERNMENT

Detail of the Grenadian Parliament Building.

GRENADA'S ROAD TO self-government began at the turn of the 20th century. This period was characterized by racial prejudice, labor unrest, and the emergence of dominant political leaders.

The British ruled Grenada as a crown colony. The governor was the head of government, assisted by a legislative council of nominated members. In the 1920s some council members could be voted in by residents who met strict property qualifications. These "unofficial" council members were expected to support any laws proposed by the governor.

Today Grenada's system of government is that of a parliamentary democracy. Its workings closely follow the British system of governing. The prime minister is the head of the government, which has three branches—executive, legislative and judicial. All Grenadians aged 18 and above are allowed to vote.

Former prime minister Herbert Blaize (*right*) with former British prime minister Margaret Thatcher (*left*).

Former prime minister Herbert Blaize with his wife after he became prime minister.

To protect their interests, the professional classes and the planters formed associations that had links to the government. The farm laborers and other workers turned to organized labor movements. These grew in strength, led successful strikes, and eventually developed into political parties.

FEDERATION FAILS

The movement toward self-government became stronger in the 1920s. It was often led by men who had served in the British West India Regiment during World War I.

One of the early leaders of Grenada was T. Albert Marryshow. He gathered a group of middle-class Grenadians of color who wanted a federation of Caribbean states to replace crown colony rule, and he formed the Representative Government Association in 1918.

Similar movements took place on most of the smaller British-ruled islands. All demanded to have some say in local government. Islanders wanted at least some members of their legislative assemblies to be elected from the local population. Many also supported a political union of the West Indies colonies. There was a brief attempt at a federation of Grenada and nine other states in 1958, but the federation dissolved, and Grenada became a British associated state in 1967.

UNIONS

Many unions emerged in the British colonies. Affiliated to British labor unions, these unions had the support of the British Labour Party. Various political

On January 3, 1958, Grenada joined nine other Caribbean states to form the West Indies Federation. Its partners were Antigua and Barbuda, Barbados, Dominica, Jamaica, Montserrat, Saint Kitts-Nevis-Anguilla, Saint Lucia, Trinidad and Tobago, and Saint Vincent and the Grenadines. The federation did not have full self-government, because the governor-general was appointed by Great Britain. The governor-general appointed the members of the Council of State and had the right to veto bills. Members of the federal House of Representatives were elected, and they chose their prime minister.

But the federation was short-lived, surviving for only three years before conflict between its two largest states, Jamaica and the archipelago state of Trinidad and Tobago, and the rest of the federation killed it. Bauxite mining on Jamaica and oil exports from Trinidad boosted the economies of these two countries, and their leaders were afraid that the poorer islands would be a drain on their economies. Jamaica left the federation in 1961. It was quickly followed by Trinidad and Tobago. The federation was dissolved soon after. An attempt by Barbados to hold the remaining states together failed because the smaller islands were afraid of being dominated by Barbados.

parties were formed from these unions during this period. Their common aim was to improve the lives of their people through education, social welfare, and better economic conditions. But achieving independence was the most important goal. Because their campaign platforms were similar, the success or failure of a party was often dependent on the charisma of its leaders.

One prominent union leader was Eric Matthew Gairy, an elementary-school teacher. He rose to prominence when he organized a successful strike in 1951 that forced the British governor to negotiate. He became a leader in both the independence and labor movements. His Grenada United Labour Party (GULP) was strongly supported by the working class and farmers. In the 1962 election, however, the GULP lost to the Grenada National Party, led by Herbert Blaize. Blaize had campaigned for unity with Trinidad and Tobago. But in 1967, after the prime minister of Trinidad, Eric Williams, rejected the idea of any union, the GULP and Gairy were returned to power.

ROAD TO SELF-GOVERNMENT

In 1940 one of Britain's goals was to help its colonies achieve self-government through universal suffrage. It began to free colonies in Asia, Africa, and the Middle East.

In Grenada every adult was allowed to vote for members of the Legislative Assembly, which later became the lower house of the Parliament of Grenada. At first, elected members on the executive council were given the responsibility of heading a ministry. When most government ministers were elected members of the assembly, the executive council effectively became a proper governing cabinet of ministers responsible to Parliament. This transition was achieved in all the crown colonies by 1956. Self-government occurred when the leader of the party with the greatest number of elected members became the chief minister and took over as governor. Britain continued to be responsible for the island's foreign policy and defense. When these functions were given to the island government, full independence was attained.

Supporters of Herbert Blaize's New National Party at a campaign rally in 1990.

BRITISH-STYLE GOVERNMENT

All the crown colonies adopted a British-style government. In Grenada the Queen of England is still the head of state, represented by a governor-general who is appointed to the office. Real political power is held by the prime minister, who is head of the government and leader of the party with the greatest number of seats in the lower house of Parliament. He presides over a cabinet of ministers.

There are two houses of Parliament: The lower house, or the House of Representatives, has 15 members elected to five-year terms, and the upper house, or Senate, has 13 members appointed by the governor-general. Seven of the senators are appointed on the advice of the prime minister, three on the advice of the leader of the official opposition, and three on the advice of the prime minister in consultation with organizations that the senators are selected to represent. The president of the Senate is selected from among the senators. All Grenadians over 18 years of age are eligible to vote.

The Parliament Building is situated in the capital, Saint George's.

REVOLUTION

When Grenada gained independence on February 7, 1974, Eric Gairy became the first prime minister. In 1979, while Gairy was overseas, a group of armed rebels overthrew him in a bloodless coup. Their leader, Maurice Bishop, became the prime minister of the new People's Revolutionary Government of Grenada. Bernard Coard, the deputy leader, became the minister of finance. Bishop's early rule saw an improvement in the lives of Grenadians.

But then he was influenced by Cuban president Fidel Castro and adopted a communist-style government. He suspended the constitution and invited Cuban advisers to Grenada. There was no longer any press freedom under his rule, and the prison was packed with political prisoners. His communist alignments made the United States and other Caribbean nations uneasy. At the same time, there was a struggle for power between Bishop and the more left-wing members of his party.

Former prime minister Maurice Bishop came to power by means of a coup.

In October 1983 the hard-liners mounted a military coup and put Bishop under house arrest. Thousands of Bishop's supporters gathered at Fort George to demand his release. The army opened fire on the crowd and killed about 40 people. Bishop and several of his friends and advisers were then taken out and executed. The government imposed a four-day curfew with orders to shoot on sight anyone found on the streets without permission.

A meeting of the Organisation of Eastern Caribbean States (OECS) was held, and it was agreed that American help should be sought.

SIX-DAY INVASION

On October 25, 1983, at the request of the governor-general, a combined force of the OECS and the United States invaded Grenada. In the fighting, 70 Cubans, 42 Americans, and 170 Grenadians died. The Americans quickly installed an interim government and restored the island's constitution. Elections were held in December 1985.

This election brought the New National Party (NNP) to power. The NNP was a coalition of three political parties, with Herbert Blaize as its leader. It

The U.S. Army unloading its weapons at the Point Salines Airport just before the invasion.

won 14 of the 15 seats in the House of Representatives. The coalition did not last very long, as the elected members soon resigned in protest against the manner in which Prime Minister Blaize handled certain issues.

In January 1989, at a party convention, Blaize was deposed as party leader and his place taken by Keith Mitchell, general secretary of the party and minister of communications and works. Blaize then formed a new party called The National Party (TNP). But Blaize's term in office was troubled by severe illness and other difficulties.

Opposition members in Parliament pressed for new elections, and Mitchell threatened to call a vote of no confidence in the government. There was unrest—civil servants were angry that salary increases that had been promised were not received, and unions and workers went on strike. Meanwhile, Blaize's health deteriorated, and he died in December 1989, just before elections were due to be called.

THE 1990 ELECTIONS

In March 1990, Grenadians went to the polls once more. This time they had five parties to choose from. The National Democratic Congress (NDC), led by Nicholas Brathwaite, won seven seats, one short of a majority. A new government was formed when TNP leader Ben Jones allied his party with the NDC. An elected member of the GULP also defected and joined the NDC.

In the June 1995 elections, the NNP, headed by Keith Mitchell, won eight seats, the NDC (now headed by George Brizan) won five, and the GULP under leader Jerry Seales won two seats. Although the next election was due to be held in October 2000, Prime Minister Mitchell called snap elections in January 1999 after two members of his ruling NNP crossed over and joined the opposition in November 1998. The NNP won the election and remained in power until the opposition NDC, led by Tillman Thomas, took over the reins of government in a convincing victory in 2008.

There are now four major political parties: the New National Party, the National Democratic Congress, the People's Labor Movement, and the Grenada United Labor Party.

The New National Party's campaign slogan in the 1990 elections was "It's Time to Settle Down."

OPERATION URGENT FURY

Several conditions precipitated the action of the United States and the OECS against Grenada. After the assassination of Maurice Bishop, the military council took control of the island, but there was utter chaos in the streets. The United States was also concerned that the Cuban-built Point Salines International Airport (now called the Maurice Bishop International Airport) would be put to military use, with Grenada becoming a missile base for the Cubans. The presence of some American medical students studying at Saint George's Medical School provided the needed excuse, and the invasion was ordered on the strength of protecting these students from the unstable situation.

On October 25, 1983, 21 helicopters from the aircraft carrier Guam landed on the beach near Pearls Airport on the eastern side of the island. There was token resistance and anti-aircraft fire, but this was quickly silenced. Another landing of helicopters farther south near the town of Grenville met with little resistance. Grenadians waved to the invading forces and welcomed them as liberators. By October 31 the Americans had gained complete control of the island, and the six-day war was over. Some members of the People's Revolutionary Government escaped, but most of them voluntarily surrendered.

KEEPING THE PEACE

Grenada's judicial system, like the rest of its government, is modeled after that of Britain's. Grenada is a member of the Eastern Caribbean Supreme Court, which is composed of regional courts that are overseen by the Privy Council in England. An associate judge resides in Grenada.

Judges are appointed to the Supreme Court by a governmental body. The lower courts are under the control of magistrates who are also appointed. The crime rate in Grenada is low, and often the only matter that the courts deal with is petty theft.

Grenada has no army. Peace in the country is enforced by the Royal Grenada Police Force, which is led by a police commissioner. After the U.S. intervention in 1983, instructors from Britain and Barbados trained a new police force to ensure that there would be adequate security after the foreign troops departed.

The Royal Grenada Police Force.

For the purpose of local administration, the island of Grenada is divided into six parishes. Beginning with the parish of Saint George in the southwest and moving clockwise, they are Saint John, Saint Mark, Saint Patrick, Saint Andrew, and Saint David. Saint George is home to 37,000 people and is where the capital and the port of Saint George's is situated. It is the most urbanized and richest parish.

More than 8,000 people live in the parish of Saint John. The main town is Gouyave, a major fishing area. The main attractions in Saint John are the Belvidere and Dougaldston estates, where bananas, cocoa, nutmeg, and other spices are grown. There is a large processing station where nutmeg and mace are prepared for shipment.

Saint Mark is the smallest parish, with a population of just under 4,000 people. Fishing and agriculture are the major industries. Grenada's highest peak, Mount Saint Catherine, is located in this parish. Saint Patrick in the north is an especially historic parish. It is where Amerindian petroglyphs have been found and where the Caribs leaped to their deaths in 1653 rather than surrender to the French. Many old homes and plantation houses have been restored to their original beauty there. Saint Andrew is the largest producer of export crops—cocoa, nutmeg, and bananas. The main town of Grenville holds a Rainbow City Festival every August, a celebration of the arts and crafts of the region. Saint David is home to about 11,000 people and is the last known habitat of the endangered Grenada dove. La Sagesse Nature Center offers visitors hiking trails through an old wooded estate and tours of a mangrove estuary.

ECONOMY

A man feeding sugarcane into a sugarcane juice machine.

W ITH ITS BEAUTIFUL BEACHES, mountain scenery, and tropical climate, Grenada is a very popular vacation spot for the growing number of tourists who arrive by air and by sea. It is not surprising, therefore, that tourism and services has become the most important sector of Grenada's economy.

The service sector makes up more than 76 percent of the country's economy, with tourism alone accounting for more than 35 percent. Tourism is also the largest earner of foreign exchange. Industry, especially textiles and construction, is next in importance, accounting for 18 percent of the gross domestic product (GDP). Agriculture, which historically was the most important economic sector from the time of the early French settlers who cultivated indigo and tobacco, now makes up a little more than 5 percent of the GDP. The three most important crops are nutmeg, bananas, and cocoa, which were introduced to the country in the 18th century.

Right: Builders working to construct a factory.

A trading schooner brings produce to markets in the bigger cities.

AGRICULTURE

Sugarcane was an important crop in Grenada in the 18th century. Power for crushing the sugarcane came from windmills and water mills. When sugarcane lost its economic value, other crops were cultivated.

In 1714 agricultural production was diversified to include cocoa, coffee, and cotton. In 1782 Sir Joseph Banks, the botanical adviser to King George III of England, introduced nutmeg to Grenada. The island's soil was ideal for growing the spice, and because it was closer to Europe than the Dutch East Indies, Grenada became an important source of spices for European traders.

In the late 19th century, coconuts and spices such as cloves and cinnamon were grown, as were avocados, breadfruits, papayas, mangoes, and five-finger fruits (also known as starfruits). Bananas became an important cash crop after Hurricane Janet hit the island in 1955. Because bananas can be

A factory worker airing cocoa beans. Cocoa beans are grown lower down the hillsides in areas of medium rainfall, while nutmeg is grown in areas that receive the greatest rainfall.

harvested seven to nine months after planting, farmers could earn money quickly while they waited for their devastated crops to recover.

Hurricane Ivan in 2004, however, wiped out the banana crop and severely damaged the other crops, including many nutmeg trees that were more than 100 years old. Grenada's agriculture industry has only recently recovered from this devastation.

SPICES

Grenada produces one-third of the world's supply of nutmeg. Nutmeg is an important ingredient in the flavoring of drinks, sauces, preserves, and other foods. The nutmeg tree is a tropical evergreen that can grow very tall, up to a height of 60 feet (18 m). It takes eight years for a nutmeg tree to fully mature, but fruit production increases each year. The fruit is round and yellow and

Spices are an important part of Grenada's export crops: (*top left to right*) clove, tonka bean, cinnamon, mace; (*bottom left to right*) cacao, pepper, coffee, and nutmeg.

appears year-round, but the harvest is especially bountiful from February to April and from August to October.

When the fruit is mature, it splits open to reveal a dark brown shell that contains the nutmeg. The shell is covered by a bright red, lacy membrane called mace. The mace is stripped from the shell and dried separately. It is a spice on its own and is also used by the pharmaceutical industry. Nutmeg and mace generate almost 40 percent of Grenada's revenue from export crops. Nutmeg is so important to Grenada that it is an emblem on the country's flag. Indonesia is the world's only other large producer of nutmeg.

Grenada also produces many other spices—allspice (the dried berry of the pimento tree), bay leaves, hot and sweet peppers, cinnamon, cloves, ginger, and vanilla.

Fishermen pulling their nets out to sea. Smaller schools of fish such as jack, couvalli, and bonita are caught with seine nets near the shore.

FISHING

Fish are plentiful around the coral reefs that surround Grenada. Fishermen who take their boats out during the traditional "ocean season" from November to June bring in tuna, kingfish, flying fish, and dolphin fish. This accounts for about half of the year's catch. For the rest of the year, fishermen have a good time harvesting bottom-dwelling snapper, grouper, and other tropical rockfish. Another kind of fishing involves catching shellfish, including lobsters and conchs, and turtles. White sea urchins are harvested for their eggs. The eggs are collected and put into clean sea urchin cases, then baked and sold.

The fishing industry has received a lot of foreign aid, particularly from Venezuela and Japan. This has made possible the construction of fish centers where the catch can be stored in cold rooms. Most of the catch from Carriacou and Petite Martinique is sold to exporters. There are public fish markets in Grenada, but fishermen still sell their fish directly from their landing site.

A luxurious resort in Grenada.

TOURISM

About 60 percent of the more than 200,000 tourists to the island arrive on large cruise ships that dock at the pier in Saint George's harbor, one of the most beautiful deep-water harbors in the Caribbean. When passengers disembark, they find that they are immediately in the heart of Saint George's, with all major attractions just a short distance away. A nearby vendors' market becomes a hive of activity on cruise-ship days, with stalls set up to sell food, clothing, and souvenirs. Grenada's busy international airport brings thousands more tourists by air each year. More than 50 establishments, ranging from small budget guesthouses to luxurious hotels with hundreds of rooms, provide accommodation.

SMALL INDUSTRIES

In 2003 manufacturing made up 18 percent of the country's GDP. The older industries are garment and furniture making, food and fruit preserving and canning, rum distillation, cottage industries, and cigarette production. These are still important in the country, but newer industries such as industrial gases, paints and varnishes, and flour and animal feeds are being encouraged. Besides nutmeg, cocoa, mace, and bananas and other fruit, Grenada's principal exports include vegetables, fish, flour, and clothing. Imports include food and live animals, beverages, fuel and lubricants, machinery, transportation equipment, and other manufactured goods.

Unloading grain from a cargo ship. Most imports come from the United Kingdom, the United States, and Trinidad and Tobago.

Grenada's main trading partners are the other members of the Organisation of Eastern Caribbean States (OECS), particularly Saint Vincent, Dominica, Saint Lucia, and Antigua; members of the Caribbean Community (CARICOM) such as Jamaica, Guyana, Barbados, Bahamas, and Trinidad; other Caribbean states; the European Union; the United States; and Japan.

OVER LAND AND SEA

The Maurice Bishop International Airport at Point Salines in the south of the island is Grenada's connection with the rest of the world. It is linked by air to other Caribbean states by LIAT (Leeward Islands Air Transport), the region's main air carrier, and several other smaller airline companies that operate interisland routes. SVG Air, the airline of Saint Vincent and the Grenadines, connects the islands with the mainland of Grenada. There is a small airport at Lauriston on Carriacou.

On the sea, ferries and shipping lines operate scheduled trips regularly between the many harbors of Grenada, Carriacou, and Petite Martinique, and between Grenada and the other Caribbean islands.

The Grenadian transportation network is well developed, and most of the roads, including those on Carriacou and Petite Martinique, are paved, although extremely narrow, winding, and steep. The main road on Grenada circles the island, linking Saint George's with all the coastal villages.

ENVIRONMENT

A tropical rain forest in Grenada.

GRENADA, BEING A VERY SMALL country made up of tiny islands, and yet having been colonized by humanity for a very long time (the earliest records of people living on these islands go back to the first century B.C.), has had a very large portion of its plant and animal life altered to suit the needs of people.

Much of Grenada is made up of land that has been cultivated or altered from its natural state in some way. Nonindigenous plants and animals have been introduced and flourished, often to the detriment of the native species. Intensive use of Grenada's natural resources plus poor agricultural practices, overfishing, industrialization, and urbanization have had their negative effects.

But there is now a greater awareness of the problems. Like people in many other parts of the world, Grenadians realize that they have to care for their environment, and policies have been put in place to make sure that the country's natural resources are used wisely. Grenada is also climatically vulnerable. It is located within the hurricane belt

Right: A garbage dump in Grenada. Irresponsible disposal of waste will have detrimental effects on the environment.

Grenadians are increasingly more aware of the need to protect their environment. Parks and marine areas are being protected to ensure the survival of flora and fauna alike.

A banana plantation.

and periodically suffers tremendous damage from these wild tropical storms. Furthermore, the global climate change crisis with its threat of rising sea levels could have a particular impact upon this island nation.

USING THE LAND WISELY

Agriculture is considered an important socioeconomic activity for Grenadians. The "isle of spice" produces nutmeg and other spices, such as cinnamon, clove, and bay leaf. It is famous for its bananas and cocoa. It is common to find next to a Grenadian house a garden growing cassava, plantains, pumpkins, sweet potatoes, tomatoes, and other crops meant for the household kitchen and the Saturday market.

Besides bananas, which are an important cash crop grown mainly for the local market, small farmers cultivate mangoes, coconuts, papayas, and watermelons. Grenadians also rear livestock. One can see chickens, goats, cows, and pigs in the villages. The soils of Grenada are mostly well drained and fairly fertile. The combination of good soil, a tropical climate, and high rainfall allows for productive farming. Unregulated farming has led to environmental problems, however. Grenada is a hilly country. Poor agricultural techniques have caused soil erosion and landslides.

There has been poor disposal of solid waste and the dumping of garbage into open dump sites. But farmers are now learning how they can grow their crops in environmentally sound ways. One way has been to go organic. In 2002, farmers in the Caribbean, with the encouragement of their governments and buyers in the European Union, decided to grow organic bananas in an effort to keep their industry competitive. In Grenada the River Antoine Estate, which also produces organic white rum, was a participant in this experimental organic banana-growing project.

Agricultural use of the land has encroached on Grenada's forests. The country's natural vegetation is extremely varied and is important for many of the birds and other animals that live there. It includes the elfin woodlands and cloud forests of Mount Saint Catherine, the montane forests of the mountain slopes, the rain forests of the lower elevations, the dry scrub woodland of Carriacou and Petite Martinique, and the mangrove forests and swamps of the coastline. But deforestation is a problem—just 12 percent of the land is forested, and only a tenth of this area is protected land. The increasing demand for land to grow crops has resulted in farmers' entering forested areas and clearing the land for small farm holdings.

PRESERVING THE RARE AND ENDANGERED

There are four main national parks in the country: Grand Etang, High North, Levera, and Mount Saint Catherine. The High North and Levera parks include marine areas. The World Database on Protected Areas (WDPA) reports 31 nationally recognized protected areas in Grenada. These include the important Annandale, Concord, and Mount Hope/Clabony watershed areas; the protected sites of La Sagesse, Mount Hartman Park, Lauriston Point, Sandy Island, and Maouya; the Tyrrel Bay Mangrove; and the coral reefs of White and Saline islands.

Watershed areas are fragile areas and require protection because they are the most important source of freshwater for the areas that they service. The Annandale and Concord watersheds supply water to densely populated Saint George's as well as to parts of Saint John's Parish. The Mount Hope and Clabony watershed is a catchment area for Grenville and the rest of the parish of Saint Andrews. Yet these areas have had much of their forest cover removed to make room for the growing of crops. The deforestation has caused soil erosion, increased the runoff of water, and affected the quality and quantity of the water supply.

The government is doing its best to improve management of these areas to ensure that the demands of agricultural use and the need for freshwater supply are balanced. The national parks are a refuge for Grenada's many

Grenada recently acquired a new food industry. The Grenada Chocolate Company, started in 1999 by two Americans and a Grenadian cocoa farmer, is the first real effort to create chocolate locally rather than just exporting the beans. The company claims that its chocolate is all organic, that it uses solar power, and that it believes in fair trade.

The Orinoco crocodile is endangered in Grenada.

species of birds, mammals, and reptiles, especially those that are now rare, threatened, and endangered through loss of habitat and excessive hunting. Among the endangered species are the Grenada hook-billed kite, the tundra peregrine falcon, the green sea and hawksbill turtles, the spectacled caiman, and the Orinoco crocodile.

FRESHWATER SUPPLY AND THE OCEANS

Grenada has limited freshwater supplies. The water is in great demand for domestic, agricultural, and industrial use. The country is small and mountainous. Its climate is humid and tropical, and instead of dividing the year into spring, summer, fall, and winter, people divide it into wet and dry seasons. The dry season runs from January to May, and the wet season from June to December. The mean annual rainfall is 92 inches (235 cm). This rain feeds the rivers, streams, lakes, and ponds that are the main sources of freshwater. But unless there are storage facilities in which the rainwater can be stored till needed, most of this supply flows down the steep slopes and into

SEA TURTLES IN GRENADA

Grenada's long coastline and sandy beaches provide ideal nesting sites for the leatherback, green sea, and hawksbill turtles. Each year, from March to July, hundreds of turtles climb laboriously upon these beaches in the dark of night to excavate their nests in the sand and lay their eggs.

In 2000 a conservation organization based in Grenada, Ocean Spirits, began a five-year project focusing on the protection of the marine turtles of Grenada. The turtles have become endangered through various activities. These include the poaching of the nests, the loss of nesting areas through development of the beaches and sand mining, pollution of the waters, and adults being caught in fishing nets. Both the adult turtles as well as their eggs have been a traditional source of food for the islanders.

But turtles are now protected in Grenada, and it is illegal to hunt them or take away their eggs. Ocean Spirits has tagged the turtles and followed their seasonal migrations from Caribbean waters back to their feeding grounds in the cooler waters as far away as Canada, the UK, and West Africa. In 2003 the group counted 586 nests laid on Levera Beach, the main nesting site in Grenada, and there are hopeful signs that the number of nesting turtles is on the increase.

Ocean Spirits continues to conduct extensive research on the turtles, in which young international volunteers participate. It also manages an education program that has involved hundreds of students from secondary schools in Grenada, teaching young Grenadians that they must become the protectors of these sea creatures that depend upon them for the survival of their species.

the sea. As mentioned elsewhere in this chapter, there are a few watershed areas—Annandale, Concord, and Mount Hope and Clabony.

These are protected areas. There is also some groundwater in the northwest part of Grenada Island. Environmental concerns relating to the supply of freshwater have to do with the quality as well as the quantity of this limited supply. The increasing demand from farmers for agricultural land has caused many of them to enter the diminishing forested areas and clear the land for planting. This has caused deforestation of the island and soil erosion, as the cleared land allows for greater water runoff to occur, resulting in the fertile topsoil being washed into rivers and streams and carried into the ocean. In addition, opening up more land for human use creates more pollution of the streams and the rivers. This further reduces the amount of freshwater available.

Pollution of the coastal waters is another environmental issue that the government of Grenada has been concerned about. The coastal waters and reefs are polluted with solid waste and other debris. Annual cleanups of the reefs and beaches turn up a lot of junk such as plastic bottles and food containers. Cruise and commercial ships that use Grenada's sea lanes and dock in its ports have to be careful of how they get rid of their solid wastes. They are required to dispose of their waste in an environmentally careful manner, but monitoring this has not been easy.

TOURISM AND THE ENVIRONMENT

The tourism industry and its related service industries is the biggest segment of the Grenadian economy. But tourism is a double-edged sword—though this industry brings much needed money to the country, it has also had a major negative impact on the environment. To accommodate the thousands of people who come here to enjoy the tropical climate, beautiful beaches, and clear waters, many hotels and resorts have been built. Environmentalists are concerned that the government is selling off too much of its land to foreigners interested in developing resorts for tourists. Those who argue that tourism is bad for the environment point to the heavy cost to the land of

When a Grenada dove is flushed from a perch, it will fly to the ground and walk away. It probably evolved at a time when there were no ground predators to threaten it, but now it is prey to mongooses, rats, and feral cats.

overdevelopment of hotels and resorts, the degradation of beaches, damage to the coral reefs, and the increasing use of plastics and other litter that people leave behind.

One very controversial project is a luxury resort planned for an area known as the Mount Hartman National Park. This area in the southwestern part of the main island is the primary habitat of the Grenada dove, Grenada's national bird. The dove, which is endemic to Grenada, is an endangered species. There are only 100—200 of these birds left in the world. The national park was established in 1994 as a refuge for the dove, but the government has changed its laws to enable the sale of the land to the developer of the resort. Naturally this has caused an outcry among both local and international birders and conservationists.

In addition to threatening the survival of the Grenada dove, this resort project has other controversial aspects to it. A bridge linking Mount Hartman with nearby Hog Island, considered a national landmark, has local residents concerned about the possible degradation of the marine environment and the mangrove forests. Mangroves are extremely salt-tolerant trees that grow in the intertidal areas along the coast. Many types of fish lay their eggs in stands of mangrove trees so that the young are protected from larger fish as they grow to adulthood. This has great significance for the fishermen and their families, as about 70 percent of the species that are being fished in Grenada are nurtured in this environment. Destruction of the mangroves could result in a depletion of fishing stocks.

There are some people, however, both in government and in the tourism industry, who believe that tourism can be successfully promoted while being environmentally friendly. In fact, ecotourism is one way of finding a middle ground—it attracts an increasing number of people who love to visit

Tourists hiking through the jungle interior to Royal Mount Carmel Waterfall.

ecologically fragile and pristine areas around the world and are concerned about doing this in an environmentally friendly manner. Some travel companies promote ecotourism by offering visitors tours that feature hiking and walking in the forests, visits to Grenada's beautiful national parks and waterfalls, and opportunities to witness the varied wildlife of the island.

For example, a large resort near Levera Beach, which is a very important breeding ground for leatherback turtles in the Caribbean region, says it aims to protect the turtle population. One way it plans to do this is by raising awareness about turtle conservation among Grenadians (turtles are a source of food for the local population) as well as among the visitors who stay at the resort.

Another large and ultraluxurious resort in the south of the island, on Grand Anse Beach, presents itself as being environmentally conscious. Among other green initiatives, it does not use chlorine in its swimming pools (chlorine is harmful to the environment). It buys food that is grown locally and organically, composts its kitchen and garden wastes, has its own vegetable and herb garden, uses solar energy, and makes its own freshwater with a desalination plant that removes salt from seawater.

Sailing is another important activity in Grenada that impacts upon the environment. Many local residents are keen sailors, and the island's tropical waters and deep and sheltered harbors attract sailors from all over the world. The development of mooring, yachting facilities, and marinas contributes much to the economy of the country and to the lifestyle of the people.

Through legislation and education, the government is making sure that those involved in developing and maintaining marinas where motorboats

Two cruise ships docked at Saint George's.

and sailboats can be docked take steps to protect the environment. This includes cleaning up the lagoons where marinas are located, installing docks that have as little impact on the environment as possible, monitoring the dumping of wastes, and ensuring that boat repairs do not cause toxic chemicals to enter and pollute the waters. Increasingly, special mooring facilities are being built and improved so that boats in the lagoons are able to tie onto them, thus removing the need to drop their anchors onto the seabed, an action that damages the marine environment.

PRESERVING THE CORAL REEFS

Grenada has an extensive network of coral reefs. Scuba diving is an important segment of the tourism industry, and there are numerous dive sites just off the shores of the islands. *Carriacou* is Arawak for "island of reefs." Again, tourism is an important factor in the health of these reefs, and its impact can be both good and bad for this environment. The reefs are very fragile, and while they take a very long time to grow, they can be damaged in an instant

Grenadians are becoming increasingly aware of the need to protect their coral reefs.

by a carelessly dropped anchor or chain from a boat or even by a diver who comes into contact with them.

There is growing awareness among Grenadians that it is important to preserve this habitat not just because it is a big money earner for the country but also because our environment has to be cared for and not depleted through carelessness and greed. Grenada's reef environment is protected, and it is illegal to remove any corals, sponges, or other reef life from these waters. A sporting and fishing license is required for fishing in the waters.

The Grenada Scuba Diving Association organizes regular cleanups of dive areas, marine parks, and beaches. Commonly found items are plastic food containers and cups, bottles, and discarded fishing lines.

CLIMATE CHANGE

The issue of climate change is one that has great significance for Grenada, as it is made up of a number of small islands in the Caribbean. What the world's

UNDERWATER SCULPTURE PARK

In 2006 sculptor Jason de Caires Taylor created the world's first underwater sculpture park in Moliniere Bay ,a little north of Saint George's. There are now more than 60 sculptures in this area, which is part of a national marine park. The sculpture Grace Reef *is made up of 16 statues cast from a local Grenadian woman.* Vicissitudes, *another sculpture, depicts 26 life-size children holding hands in a circle. The sculptures, made of cement, are submerged in the clear and shallow waters of the bay where they can be easily viewed by divers, snorkelers, and visitors in glass-bottomed boats.*

They are intended to focus attention on the issue of overuse of the marine environment by diving, boating, and fishing; the fragility and beauty of the coral reef; and the relationship between art and nature. The bay and its reefs were badly hit by Hurricane Ivan in 2004. The sculptures provide a habitat for marine life and form the foundations of an artificial reef. As they lie on the seabed, they will continue to interact with their environment and be colonized by living coral and other marine life, which will help rejuvenate the waters of the bay. Taylor, born in 1974 to an English father and a Guyanese mother, is an avid diver, underwater naturalist, and photographer.

climate experts basically agree upon is that a strong warming trend noticed since the 1970s has been in large part the work of mankind. Although many factors have an impact on the world's climate, such as the way the oceans and the atmosphere interact, the changes in the earth's orbit, and changes in the energy received from the sun and volcanic eruptions, it is human activity and the amount of greenhouse gases (mainly carbon dioxide and the water vapor that it produces) that have mainly been responsible for this warming trend.

For Grenada, one major concern of climate change lies in its impact on sea levels. The Intergovernmental Panel on Climate Change (IPCC), made up of scientists from around the world, has estimated that in the past century sea levels rose by 7 inches (17 cm) because of the increase in the earth's temperature. Further rises in sea levels can be expected, and it has been predicted that by the end of this century the sea level could rise by anything

Whitespotted filefish among corals. Coral reefs are easily affected by the temperature and acidity of the water.

from 7 to 23 inches (18 to 59 cm). This would cause the loss of a significant portion of the country's coastline through flooding and destroy the mangrove forests, the harbor, and much of the livable space. In addition, scientists have said that increased levels of carbon dioxide in the atmosphere are affecting the coral reefs in two ways: through the rise in the temperature of the water and through an increase in its acidity. Increased environmental stress causes the corals to be bleached (lose their color) and become weaker and more prone to disease. When carbon dioxide dissolves in seawater, making it more acidic, it affects the way in which the coral reef is formed. Reefs are made up of calcium carbonate, produced by tiny creatures called coral polyps. Researchers have found that the increased acidity of the water slows the polyps' production of calcium carbonate.

Some studies have also shown that reef-forming coral cannot survive in water that is too acidic. As the reefs are a habitat for many species of fish and other marine life, the dying of the coral would affect the entire ecosystem of the reef. The destruction of this ecosystem, besides removing a beautiful natural environment for our enjoyment, would have dire effects on the economy of the country, affecting the fishing and tourism industries and the people as a whole.

A third whammy that climate change will probably deliver to the small nation of Grenada is in the area of hurricanes. There has been evidence since the 1970s that a correlation exists between the number of intense tropical storms and increases in the temperature of the sea. It is very likely that the increase in greenhouse gases has contributed to the rise in the sea surface temperatures in regions of hurricane formation. The IPCC said in its 2007 report that it is "more likely than not" that there is a human contribution to the increased intensity of hurricanes since the 1970s. The IPCC also said that "it is likely that future tropical storms will become more intense, with larger peak wind speeds and more heavy precipitation associated with ongoing increases of tropical [sea surface temperatures]."

As a very small country, Grenada can do little to fight the global warming that is the result of climate change. As part of the Caribbean community of nations, however, it has joined its neighbors in planning for the effects of climate change. This has included monitoring and analyzing climate and sea-level trends, identifying areas that are particularly vulnerable, and developing a management plan for an effective response to the impact of climate change. In addition, the government is participating in United Nations environmental efforts and negotiations such as the Kyoto Protocol and has begun imposing environmental levies on cruise-ship passengers to fund efforts to reduce beach erosion and control tourism-related pollution. Grenada is also a party to many other international environmental treaties including those on biodiversity, endangered species, whaling, and ozone protection.

A woman walking among damaged yachts in the marina after Hurricane Ivan.

GRENADIANS

Two girls pose in front of a mural.

6

MORE THAN 80 PERCENT OF ALL Grenadians are of African descent, while the remainder of the population consists of small percentages of East Indians, Europeans, and other races.

When the Spanish first arrived in the Caribbean, they found three major groups of people, all of whom had come from South America. The Ciboneys lived on the northwestern tip of Cuba and Hispaniola. The Bahamas, Greater Antilles, and Trinidad were dominated by the Arawaks, while the Caribs were found on the Virgin Islands, many islands of the Lesser Antilles, and the northwestern tip of Trinidad.

The Arawaks told the Spanish that they had arrived on the islands after the Ciboneys, and that the Caribs had subsequently chased them away. There were no written records, so the Spanish accounts and archaeological evidence are the only basis of truth for these assertions. But archaeologists believe that they are true.

INDIGENOUS PEOPLE

The Ciboneys were the most primitive group. They lived in rock shelters and caves

Right: A Grenadian man selling steel drums in a tourist market near the Carenage.

A vendor proudly holding up her handmade dolls.

by the coast, and they survived by collecting shellfish, fruit, and herbs and by hunting and fishing. They wore minimal clothing, painted their bodies, and used stone tools.

The Arawaks and the Caribs had a more advanced way of life. In addition to hunting and fishing, they cultivated the land, wore handwoven clothing, made pottery, lived in huts, and built boats. They used a sophisticated method of cultivation that required burning the forest and bush.

They grew cassavas, yams, sweet potatoes, and many other crops. To supplement their diet, they hunted birds, iguanas, snakes, and small insects, and fished for a variety of marine life. They loved eating the eggs and flesh of green turtles. Food was cooked by simmering ingredients in a pot. These eating habits have continued to this day—the green turtle is a delicacy, and a "one-pot" meal of vegetables and meat is often eaten.

The Caribs were seafaring people and great boat builders. More warlike than the Arawaks, they had some success resisting the European powers.

To assume that Grenadians are only African is too narrow a view. Many of them have English, French, Dutch, Portuguese, Polish, Amerindian, or Chinese ancestors.

The Arawaks and the Caribs lived relatively healthy lives until the Europeans arrived, bringing new diseases with them. They were not immune to these diseases and fell ill. This, plus the hard labor that the Europeans forced them to perform, led to their extermination. When Columbus first arrived in the Caribbean in 1492, there were about 750,000 Amerindians. Within 20 years they were almost all dead.

SLAVERY

The Europeans imported slaves from the west coast of Africa to replace the labor they had lost, especially on islands where sugar had been planted. The slave trade reached its peak in the 17th and 18th centuries. The Dutch, the French, and the British established settlements and warehouses along the west coast of Africa where slaves were held in preparation for their arduous journey across the Atlantic. Britain was the main slaving nation.

Slaves who were shipped from West Africa were packed into ships like sardines in a can. They watched as their companions fell ill, suffered, and died. Some threw themselves overboard in desperation.

Between 1690 and 1807, British traders brought over more than 2.5 million slaves to the Caribbean and Spanish America. Sometimes an entire shipload of slaves would be sold to one planter, but it was more common for them to be sold at a public auction. In this way families were broken up, and slaves coming from a single tribe were deliberately separated from each other. When all the less than able-bodied slaves had been sold, the healthy ones were often sold at a "scramble." The slaves were put in an enclosure, and at the sound of a bell, the buyers would rush in and scramble for whomever they could get.

PLANTATION LIFE

Life on the plantation was hard. A slave had to work extremely long hours and received poor food and little clothing. Many of them died of exhaustion or illness, only to be replaced by more slaves. By law, a Grenadian slave was entitled to a bit of land to grow, or "ground," provisions. Slaves were also entitled to a house in which to live, a weekly ration of salt and salted fish,

A farmer harvesting his fruit. Bananas became an important crop after the hurricane of 1955.

and an annual quota of clothing. More often than not, however, the slaves got nothing in return for their toil.

Many rebelled by running away to join Maroon communities in the undeveloped interior of the island, malingering in the fields, or damaging the property of their masters. The Maroons were runaway slaves who had escaped their masters and hid in the forests.

By the 1750s almost 90 percent of the people on sugar-growing islands were slaves. By the end of the 18th century, slaves had to do every kind of task conceivable—they were laborers, gang drivers, and overseers. In towns they could become skilled craftsmen. Their situation ranged from total bondage to comparative freedom. The lives of the people, especially the slaves, improved dramatically when the plantation system disintegrated in the 1820s.

Many religious and social organizations were formed to improve their lives, and most of them provided religious instruction to the slaves. These included the Society for the Education of the Poor, which started the Central School in Saint George's for the children of the free blacks; the Society for the Promotion of Christian Knowledge; and the Grenada District Committee. The clergy, all paid by the government, visited the estates and gave instruction to the slaves. It was at this time that many of them converted to Christianity.

INDENTURED LABOR

After emancipation in 1834, planters relied on labor brought in from other countries. Indians, Portuguese, Maltese, and even Africans arrived on the island. The free Africans who came as indentured immigrants later joined their fellow tribespeople who had arrived before them in forming villages and cultivating the land.

Most of the Indians came from Calcutta (now known as Kolkata) and Madras (now called Chennai). They saved up their money, and when many returned to India later, they brought home sizable savings. Others migrated to Trinidad and British Guyana. Many of them converted to Christianity from Hinduism and Islam.

After the slaves were freed, many worked on their own small plots of land or cultivated a shared area with other former slaves.

THE PEOPLE TODAY

Grenadians today are very much a product of their history. The experience of slavery has resulted in a tendency to reject authority and all its symbols, as well as a disdain for manual labor and working in the hot sun. From the French and the English, the Grenadians gained religion and education, as well as a legal and political structure. The French influence today is limited to the names of people and places and some expressions that have lingered in daily language. English has given Grenadians a means to gain access to global opportunities and become a part of the world at large.

Politically and economically, the United States plays an extremely important role in Grenadian life. Its proximity has made it easy for Grenadians to be exposed to American values and culture. In addition to roti, peas, and rice, Grenadians eat fast food; they wear T-shirts and jeans; are attracted by brand-named goods; and watch American television. Their sports idols are not just local cricket players but also American basketball stars.

Grenadian schoolchildren. Grenadians are a product of their colorful history and have been influenced by many cultures.

THE SISTER ISLANDS

While the people who live on Grenada's sister islands consider themselves to be a part of Grenada, they are proud of their special identities as Kayaks (as the Carriacouans call themselves) and Petite Martiniquans. The earliest settlers on Carriacou were French turtle hunters and fishermen. They were quickly joined by migrants from the neighboring French island of Guadeloupe who had left their homes when their crops were destroyed by ants.

As on the island of Grenada, the evidence of French occupation on Carriacou is clear in the names of its villages—Ma Chapelle, L'Esterre, Belair, and Bellevue. Sugar and cotton plantations were later developed, and hundreds of slaves were imported to help cultivate the crops. Carriacouans have a unique culture that is a blend of European—English, French, and Scottish—and African traditions. While much of the original culture has been diluted on other islands, the people of Carriacou have retained many of their traditions. This can be attributed to the fact that most of the original property holders were absentee planters. The slaves were therefore less restricted and able to retain more of their traditions than those on Grenada. This is seen in the survival of the Big Drum ceremony, folk beliefs and dances, and special celebrations such as the Boat Launching ceremony, Carnival, and the Parang Festival.

Petite Martinique, like Carriacou, was settled by the French. The people of Petite Martinique have always been known for their proud and independent lifestyle, which is intimately linked to the sea. The men are either fishermen or sailors, while the women tend the crops and are used to fending for themselves and their children during the long absences of their menfolk. Petite Martinique has a reputation for being a smuggler's paradise. This was probably because the independent lifestyle and ability to sail to other ports led the islanders to smuggling as a simple way of obtaining items that they needed.

Underlying this is their African heritage, evident in their speech and rhythmic movements. Grenadians also identify with the rest of the Caribbean world, which shares this same mix of influences.

LIFESTYLE

Grenadians at a market.

CHAPTER 7

THANKS TO BALMY TROPICAL WINDS, warm temperatures, and a relaxed attitude, life on Grenada moves to a slower rhythm than that of the United States. Visitors to the island quickly adapt to this leisurely pace, and much has been said about the Caribbean islanders' lack of a sense of urgency.

Villages are strung out along the main island highway, houses clinging to the hillsides and congregating where there is sufficient space to form little communities. Each village has at least one church, a school or

A boy taking a break from work.

two, the village green where local soccer matches are played, and numerous corner drink and grocery shops.

The church is an important anchor in Grenadian life. All life events—a birth in the family, marriage, and death—are celebrated there. As in many other parts of the world, however, the old traditions have less influence on people today.

VILLAGE RHYTHMS

Grenada's villages are mainly fishing and farming communities where life is not ruled by the clock. Fishermen put their boats out in the morning and come back at the end of the day with their catch. They blow on a conch shell to announce that they have fish to sell. When a fishing boat comes in, everyone, especially the children, goes down to the beach, curious to see what the catch is.

Houses are usually simple and rectangular in shape, with two or three bedrooms, a living area, a kitchen, and a bathroom. If more space is required, a wooden shed may be added to the side. Bushes with colorful leaves and flowers are often planted in the front and serve to divide one yard from another. Vegetable gardens flourish behind the houses together with many fruit trees. A family may own some chickens along with a few goats and cows tethered to a nearby tree or post. If they have a small plot of land to farm, whole families will be engaged in agriculture.

MARKET DAY

Markets are integral to a Grenadian's life. Women cultivate vegetables for their families and take the excess to the market to sell. The market functions most of the week except Sunday, from early morning to late afternoon. It is most lively on Saturdays. The largest Saturday markets are in the towns of Saint George's and Grenville.

Stalls are often nothing more than makeshift boxes of scrap wood nailed together, topped off with large and colorful umbrellas. People gather not

Vegetables, spices, and fruit can all be found in a market.

only to shop for the items they need but also to spend time chatting with their friends. The streets are filled with groups of men and women "liming," as a Grenadian might say, meaning just standing around and relaxing with friends.

Meat and fish are sold at specialized markets such as the Melville Street Fish Market and Abattoir on Grenada Island. Women sell mainly small fish called jacks from wooden trays set upon pails full of fish. A carved-up green turtle is occasionally part of the morning's offering. Every Friday night stalls sprout on the streets of Gouyave. The vendors cook local fish delicacies in a food fair called the Gouyave Fish Festival.

TRANSPORTATION

The family car is often a small sedan, but pickups and four-wheel drives are fairly common. Bicycles and motorbikes are commonly seen on weekends, when young boys whiz down the streets on their way to the beach. Those

The bustling bus terminal in Saint George's.

without their own means of transportation walk wherever they can. For longer journeys, a taxi or a bus is indispensable.

Taxis are costly and are preferred by tourists. Most Grenadians use buses, which are actually minivans that carry up to 18 passengers comfortably. The bus is operated by a driver and his assistant, who try to get as many people in the bus as they can to maximize the revenue from each trip. Buses crammed with passengers are a common sight. As Grenada's roads are narrow and winding, a bus ride can often be a hair-raising experience.

Bus terminals are in the heart of Saint George's near Market Square and the Esplanade, and bus routes fan out from there to cover the entire island. Although there are bus stops, buses will pick up passengers anywhere along the route, even though it is illegal to do so.

GRENADIAN WOMEN

Women have always been a source of cheap unskilled and semiskilled labor in Grenada. During the days of slavery, they were field and house slaves.

Women are usually engaged in a variety of occupations outside the home.

After emancipation, they became laborers on plantations. They later worked in factories. If they did not have a job outside the home, they planted gardens and sold their extra provisions in the market to earn money.

Women are still employed in traditionally female occupations today. Many of them are in domestic service or work as seamstresses, hairdressers, and factory workers. The more educated are often teachers and nurses, or they work in the service sector, such as in tourism. A small number hold administrative and senior management positions in private companies, public service, and political office.

Grenadian women have always had the major responsibility for caring for and nurturing the family, even when the male head of the household was present. Many have to work outside the home to supplement the family income. Having their own money gives them a sense of independence, self-esteem, and power in their family and community.

The Grenadian government set up Cedars Shelter for abused women and children in 1999. This center provides temporary shelter and counseling for women and children in need of help.

THE FAMILY UNIT

Grenadians tend to be traditional and conservative in their outlook. The family unit is important, and the concept of family goes beyond immediate members to embrace extended members, close friends, and neighbors.

Most women are expected to bear children and to be responsible for their care and upbringing. Women tend to bear children at an early age. In the late 1990s the average Grenadian woman gave birth to three or four children, but the fertility rate has dropped since then to 2.23 children. Teenage pregnancies are common and often result in the young women having to leave school prematurely. Women who have no children of their own often care for the children of others. Therefore, besides their mothers, children may be raised by other close relatives, friends, or neighbors.

In return, the children are expected to look after their parents in their old age. Parents look forward to their children "doing well" and being able to financially support them. Respect for elders and sharing among the family are instilled in children when they are very young.

A TRADITIONAL GRENADIAN WEDDING

Weddings are spectacular affairs that involve ceremonies such as the dancing of the cake and dancing the flag. The bride's and the groom's wedding cakes are displayed by selected women from each side of the family who dance while holding the cakes on trays. In the same way, male dancers from both sides dance with the groom's and the bride's flags. This is a lighthearted but thrilling competition in which each dancer tries to gain supremacy, but it is

Girls learn from an early age to be independent.

finally the groom's cake and flag that must always be kept above the bride's, because he is the head of the family.

After the competition, both flags are placed above the bride's home, and everybody proceeds to church for the wedding service. The wedding reception may be held at the bride's home or, if the crowd is too large, in a hall. A procession of cars, all tooting their horns, announces the arrival of the wedding couple, and the guests file out to greet them and shower them with rice. They enter the home passing under an archway of coconut palms and accompanied by a string band. Inside, the wedding couple is greeted by their parents and led to the wedding table for a reception. There is lots of music and dancing. Once it ends, the couple pack their things into a car and drive to their new home.

RITUALS OF DEATH

The rituals that accompany a death incorporate both Christian practices and folk beliefs. The family of the deceased is responsible for the funeral preparations. During the wake, the men and boys will build the coffin in one corner of the yard, while the women and girls prepare mourning clothes, headcloths, and ribbons for the mourners. Food is prepared—usually tea or coffee with bread or biscuits, and rum. A spicy tea made from the leaves of a native bush was traditionally served, but coffee is a modern substitute.

On the day of the burial, the coffin is borne to church or the cemetery. Hymns are sung along the way. Two chairs are taken along on which to place the coffin if a change of pallbearers is required. At the entrance to the cemetery, the chairs are turned upside down to allow the spirit of the dead to leave the chairs. When the bearers are relieved of their burden, they shake out their arms to transfer the spirit back to the coffin. An evergreen tree is planted to mark the tomb. Relatives who visit after the funeral throw water and rum on it. A prayer meeting is also held after the funeral at the house where the death occurred. On that day a *saraca* (SAH-ra-ca), or special sacrificial feast, is prepared. A tombstone for the grave is not erected until enough time has passed to allow the earth to settle.

The placing of the stone requires a stone feast. The stone is first placed on the main bed in the house, and a sacrificial plate of food is placed on a table. The stone is then taken outside where it is blessed with a sprinkling of water, rum, rice, and eggs. Prayers are said before it is ceremoniously taken to the cemetery and placed on the grave. Then a Big Drum ceremony is held, followed by much feasting and dancing. The food is cooked in big pots and includes stewed peas, ground provisions (root vegetables), bananas, rolled rice, *coo-coo* (ground cornmeal cooked into a cake with coconut, salt, and water), and plenty of meat—pork, chicken, and mutton.

BIRTH

Less ceremony is involved when there is a birth in the family. With improved medical services, most women now have their babies delivered in the maternity ward of a hospital, under the care of doctors and nurses.

When births at home were the norm, especially in the villages, the delivery was taken care of by the district nurse or doctor. The father did not involve himself in the event but remained outside the room until he was called. If a birth was difficult, the woman's parents would walk around the house pouring rum and water at each corner and praying for a safe and quick delivery. The umbilical cord and afterbirth were often buried under a tree. After giving birth, the mother was not allowed to go outdoors but had to remain in the house for eight days. Tradition dictated that she had to bathe twice a day. When friends and relatives visited the family, they brought food and gifts for the mother and a silver coin for the newborn baby.

HEALTH

There are four hospitals in Grenada. The main one is the General Hospital in Saint George's. The other three are Mount Gay Hospital, also in Saint George's; Princess Alice Hospital in the parish of Saint Andrew; and Princess Royal Hospital on Carriacou. These hospitals are able to take care of most medical problems, but serious cases may be sent to the larger Caribbean island of

Barbados or to the United States. Health centers and district medical stations provide essential health care services for the rest of the rural areas. There are also homes for handicapped children and the elderly. Grenadians do not have to pay for their medical and dental treatment, which is provided by the government.

Life expectancy has improved dramatically during the past half-century as a result of better health care and a higher standard of living. Today most Grenadians expect to live into their 70s.

EDUCATION

Grenada has inherited the British system of education. Education is free and compulsory for children from 5 to 16 years of age. At the end of primary school, children take a common entrance examination. If they pass and are under the age of 16, they can continue their education in a secondary school. If they are above 16, they pursue a technical education.

Secondary school is five years during which students prepare for an examination set by the Caribbean Examination Council, after which they may move on to a preuniversity level of studies at the Grenada National College. Except for a few private ones, schools are coeducational. Young Grenadians can also choose to attend technical and vocational institutes to study agriculture, secretarial skills, drafting, auto mechanics, plumbing, and other courses. Saint George's University is the highest institution of learning in Grenada. It began as a school of medicine in 1977 but has since expanded to include arts and sciences and a school of graduate studies. Students can attend a branch of the University of the West Indies in Grenada.

A student working out math problems on a blackboard.

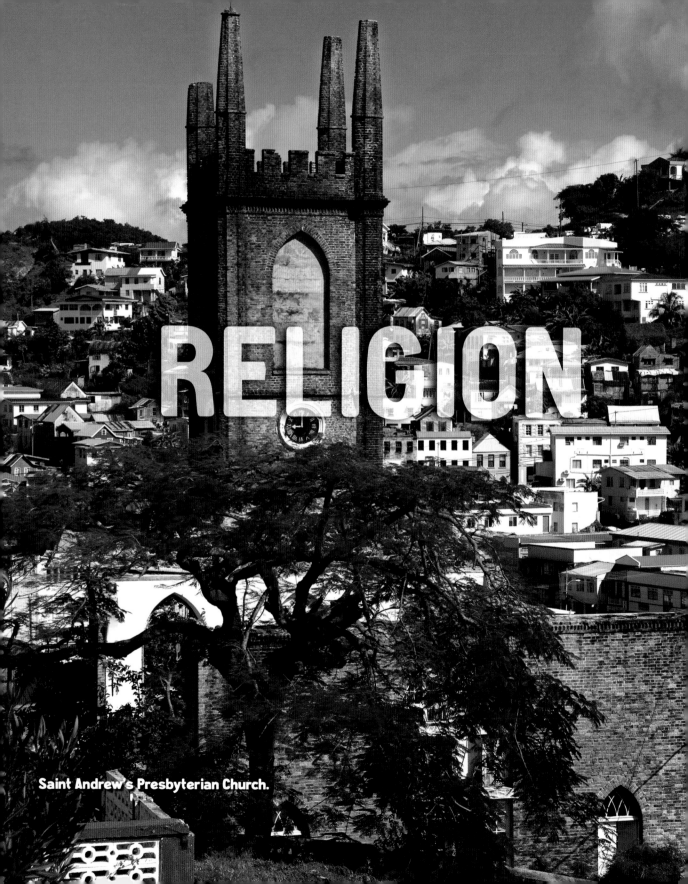

RELIGION

Saint Andrew's Presbyterian Church.

WHEN THE EUROPEANS FIRST arrived in the Caribbean, they thought that the indigenous people they encountered—the Arawaks and Caribs—had no religion. Although these people did not have a religion recognizable to the Europeans, they did have beliefs that were of a religious or supernatural nature.

The majority of Grenadians are Christian as a result of colonization by Christian Britain.

The indigenous people were animists, believing in the existence of many spirits that could interfere with or influence human life. These spirits were associated with natural elements or phenomena that they controlled. They could inhabit physical objects, which the natives worshiped, and people could be possessed by spirits. When this happened, the spirit had to be exorcized by a priest or shaman.

These people had a clear sense of what it meant to be good or bad from young. For the Caribs, it was good to be courageous and resourceful in battle, as they were a warlike people. Good behavior for the Arawaks, on the other hand, was to be gentle and peace-loving.

The Europeans tried to convert them to the Christian faith. For much of the Greater Antilles, the conquering and "civilizing" of the indigenous people was done by the Spanish. On Grenada, as on many other islands

Right: A Baptist at a prayer meeting.

85

of the Lesser Antilles, the task was undertaken by the French colonizers. However, hostilities between the French colonizers and the Caribs broke out, leading to the expulsion and extermination of all Carib people on the island of Grenada.

ARRIVAL OF THE DOMINICANS

With the French colonial government came the establishment of the Roman Catholic religion. The first Roman Catholic mission to arrive in Grenada was the Dominican order. The Dominicans were given land to help establish them in their missionary work. They were followed by the Capuchins, who in 1690 built a church in Fort Royal, then another one in the capital. An Anglican church now stands on that site.

When Grenada was ceded to the British in 1763, the British government established the Church of England (or the Anglican Church) on the island. This led to the persecution of the Roman Catholic Church until 1795. Roman

Saint Patrick's Catholic Church in Hillsborough.

Catholic relics, altars, and baptismal fonts were destroyed. The settlers on Grenada, who were mainly French, were pressured to give up their Roman Catholic faith and embrace Anglicanism. Many fled to Trinidad to escape the persecution, taking their slaves with them.

FOUR MAIN CHRISTIAN CHURCHES

By the 1800s four main Christian denominations were active in Grenada: the Anglicans, the Roman Catholics, the Methodists, and the Presbyterians, or the Church of Scotland. These churches competed for converts. The Anglican Church had the support of the colonial government and was a rich landowner. Along with the Church of Scotland, it attracted the ruling class and the planters. The Roman Catholic Church had the greatest number of working-class followers.

Saint Peter's Church.

The interior of an Anglican church in Saint George's.

The churches brought with them missionaries who set up some of the first schools in the Caribbean. The first convent and school to be founded in Grenada was Saint Joseph's Convent, established in 1876 by four nuns from Trinidad who belonged to the missionary order of Saint Joseph of Cluny.

The Sisters of Saint Joseph of Cluny also opened a school in Grenville in 1953 and run a school in the parish of Saint David. Today the antagonism among the faiths has been overtaken by a spirit of unity in which the various Christian churches live and work together.

TRADITIONAL BELIEFS

The slaves brought with them their African beliefs, but these practices were discouraged, if not banned, by the plantation owners. As a result, many African religious practices soon died. Missionaries converted the slaves to Christianity. Today the church forms an integral part of village social life.

Most islanders belong to one Christian faith or another. More than 50 percent are Roman Catholics, 14 percent are Anglicans, and another 33 percent belong to other Protestant churches. A small segment of Grenadian society belongs to other faiths. The East Indians who came to Grenada brought their own beliefs with them. Most of them were Hindu, while a small percentage were Muslims. Many converted to Christianity. There is no Hindu temple on Grenada, but there is a mosque at the southern end of the island.

Shango is an African religion that has limited influence in Grenada. Most followers of Shango also consider themselves Christians. Many of the African spirits or deities have their counterparts in the Christian saints or the Old Testament prophets. For example, the spirit Shango, who is a fierce preacher and hunter, is identified with Saint John, and Legba is associated with the devil.

Obeah, a kind of witchcraft or sorcery, is another African practice that has survived. A believer in obeah might go to an obeah practitioner to get him or her to cast a spell on an enemy. Grenadians also believe that supernatural phenomena in this world can interfere with one's life. Children are considered especially vulnerable to interference by spirits and have to be protected.

A Rastafarian. Rastafarians call one another "brother."

RASTASFARIANS

Rastafarianism, a movement that began in Jamaica in the 1930s, has spread widely throughout the Caribbean, including Grenada. Rastafarians believe that a former emperor of Ethiopia, Haile Selassie, was an incarnation of God and that his crowning was the fulfillment of a prophecy that one day someone who would unite all Africans in one nation would rise up in Africa.

Rastafarians interpret the Bible in the light of their beliefs. Although they do not marry they are faithful to their partners and frown upon infidelity and promiscuity. Some Rastafarians grow their beards, sport dreadlocks, and wear robes.

WELCOME TO

LAURISTON AIRPORT

LANGUAGE

A welcome sign painted on the wall of an airport on Carriacou Island.

CARRIACOU

MOST PEOPLE IN GRENADA CAN speak English. It is the official language of the country and is the language of instruction in schools.

When African slaves were brought over to work on the plantations, they brought with them their own languages. But laborers, overseers, and plantation owners all had to learn to communicate with and understand each other. This was achieved through a natural process of creolization of the language.

When Grenada was a French colony, the people spoke a creole that was a mixture of French and African dialect, but when the British took control of the country, Grenadians changed to a creole based on English. Today the French creole is hardly ever spoken except by some older people.

The vast majority of Grenadians speak English.

The language that is spoken in Grenada today is a testament to the country's rich history. In order to communicate with one another, plantation owners and slaves spoke a hybrid language called creole. When the French were in power French creole was spoken. English creole was adopted when the British came to power, and it is still spoken today.

CREOLE ENGLISH

There was a tendency in the past for people of the upper classes to speak Standard English and for those of the lower classes to speak a creolized dialect. This has resulted in a lingering "colonial" attitude toward language. It was a badge of good breeding and social class to speak "the Queen's English" or "BBC English" (that spoken by a British Broadcasting Corporation announcer), and to acquire a refined English accent was highly desirable.

Grenadian educator Clyde Belfon, who has made a study of the language of his people, believes that creole English rather than Standard English (the English that Grenadians learn in school) is the first language of the people. It has its own syntax, vocabulary, rhythm, and meaning. There is, however, a stigma associated with creole English—many believe that it is "bad English," the language of uneducated people.

Those who believe in the value of creole English hope that the biased "colonial" attitude is dying and that creole English as it is spoken in Grenada and many other parts of the Caribbean will eventually be recognized as a language in its own right.

Grenadians use creole English in the marketplace.

SOME COMMON EXPRESSIONS

Just now—*Don't expect something immediately*

Now for now—*Right away*

Don't make me vex—*Don't make me angry*

Don't mamaguy me—*Don't tell me a lie*

Comess—*A total confusion*

Fete—*A party*

For so—*For no reason*

Fete for so—*A party on the spur of the moment*

Like bush, like peas—*There is a lot of whatever it is*

Fete as bush—*A grand party with plenty to eat and drink*

Brango—*Spicy gossip*

Play lougarou—*Play the fool*

Sea bath—*A swim*

Lime—*Relax, hang around*

Beating mouth—*Chatting*

Farse—*Nosey*

Fire one—*Drink rum*

Me tell you—*I'm telling you*

You too sut—*You are too stupid*

Make a blow—*Buy a drink*

Study your head—*Be careful what you say or do*

Pork ah pork no beef—*Not of the best*

Don't give me a six for nine—*Don't mislead me*

The firm big—*The family has money*

Watch your case—*Be careful*

Wood have ears—*Someone may be listening*

The younger generation of Grenadians do not use French creole at all. However, many phrases and terms that they use stem from French.

THE FRENCH CONNECTION

Many place names in Grenada are French, such as *Gouyave* (Guava), *Grand Etang* (Great Lake), and *Lance aux Epines* (from *L'Anse aux Epines*, or Beach of Pines). Many words come from French and creole French. The first day of Carnival is called *jouvert* (jou-vay) from *jour ouvert*, meaning "the beginning of day." Lajabless, the she-devil that storytellers frighten little children with, comes from *la diablesse*, meaning "female devil." There are also expressions derived from French. "Well yes, oui!" is often used to express exasperation or indignation. *Bunjay*, from the expression *bon dieu*, is an exclamation of surprise or used for emphasis.

One good way to get a feel for creole English is to read *Tidal Wave,* a novel written by Clyde Belfon in both Standard English and creole English. Another book is *Snowflakes in the Sun* by Grenadian writer Jean Buffong. It is filled with the special expressions of informal Grenadian English.

THE MEDIA

About 98 percent of Grenadians above the age of 15 can read and write. With such a high literacy rate, it is no wonder that the media have a long history. An entry in the 1946 *Grenada Handbook and Directory* claimed that the *Grenadian Chronicle*, which began its publication in 1784, was "the oldest newspaper in the Western Hemisphere and the second oldest in the English-speaking world," having been established even before the *Times of London*, which began publication in 1788.

In 1915 the *Chronicle* ceased publication, giving way that year to a new newspaper, the *West Indian*. After the 1979 coup, the revolutionary government took over the paper and renamed it the *Free West Indian*. There are two independent weekly newspapers, the *Informer* and *Grenada Today*. In addition, there are many online publications.

The island's first television station was built by the Cubans when the People's Revolutionary Government was in power, but it was destroyed during the U.S. invasion. A new station was built in 1985 with American aid. Grenada Broadcasting Network shows local news, sports, and entertainment. Cable television brings major U.S. network broadcasts to the island.

A satellite dish enables Grenadians to watch U.S. television broadcasts.

ARTS

A steel drum band.

THE MUSIC OF THE CARIBBEAN— whether calypso, reggae, or soca—can be heard everywhere: on the radio, as you walk down the streets of Grenada, or from the back of a taxi or a bus. Much of the music has its roots in African folk music with drumming and strong rhythms.

Grenadians are a musical people, and this is seen in their love of dance. Many of the dances have African origins, but the French and the English also contributed to the dance heritage of Grenada.

A man playing a Caribbean mandolin. Music is an integral part of Grenadian life.

Music features prominently in Grenadian culture and can be heard everywhere. A popular form of music is known as calypso. Another distinctive sound of Grenada is made by the steel pan. Apart from music, Grenadians are also fond of dancing. Many artists in Grenada are self-taught, and a handful are internationally acclaimed.

The arts scene is thriving, with folk artists, craftspeople, and storytellers. The modern version of the storyteller is found in the theater and in the oral poetry performed in front of large crowds. Even the houses on the island are a canvas for artistic expression. Their extremely colorful exteriors display the exuberance and gaiety that people bring to self-expression.

CALYPSO

Calypso had its beginnings in Trinidad in the 18th century, and from there it spread to the rest of the region. Calypso came about when slaves working on the plantations started to sing satirical songs in French patois. It was their way of mocking their European masters and expressing their discontent. Sometimes singers would try to outdo each other in a battle of words and verbal insults. The lyrics of early calypso songs were often composed on the spot, showing the creativity and wit of the singers.

Today calypso is usually sung in English. The songs are still satirical and biting in their commentary on social and political conditions, exposing sham, pretense, and injustices on the Grenadian islands. There are often sexual innuendoes in the songs. The melody and the rhythms are similar, but the lyrics change from song to song.

A man singing passionately while playing his guitar.

Calypso competitions are an important part of the Carnival celebrations, when many singers vie for the title of Calypso King. The singers like to take on special expressive names such as Attila the Hun, King Pharaoh, Lord Executor, and Duke of Iron.

FAMOUS CALYPSO SINGERS

One famous calypso singer is Slinger Francisco, better known as the Mighty Sparrow or simply Sparrow. Born in Grenada in 1935, Sparrow moved to Trinidad with his family when he was still a little boy. The talented musician composed songs at an early age. His first public performance was in 1954, when he was 19 years old. Two years later he won the Trinidad Carnival calypso competition with his song "Jean and Dinah." He has since composed innumerable songs and produced more than 40 music albums.

Sparrow has inspired many Grenadians, who need little incentive to express the musical rhythm and creativity that seem to live in their souls. William Elcock, alias Scaramouche, is one such individual. One of a family of 12 children, Scaramouche grew up in a house made of cane straw with a leaky roof. He ran away from his family by stowing away on board a boat bound for Trinidad. In Trinidad he hung around a steel-band pan yard, eventually gaining acceptance and a job as a general helper.

Young William soon learned to play the steel drum—also known as playing pan—and became a professional, performing with a steel band. He also began to compose songs, eventually winning a calypso crown for one of his compositions. He joined the Mighty Sparrow and chose Scaramouche as his stage name because the film of that same title, starring Stewart Granger, was showing at the time.

After a short sojourn in the United States, Scaramouche returned to Grenada in 1970 and won the country's calypso crown that year. When Ronald Reagan, then president of the United States, visited Grenada in 1983, Scaramouche was chosen to sing for him. In 1994 he was picked to entertain Princess Anne of Great Britain when she was visiting the nearby Grenadine island of Mustique.

Another influential singer in Grenada is Alphonsus Cassell, who has been singing calypso for more than 20 years. Better known as Arrow, he first learned to play the ukulele, then the guitar, and after that the steel drum. Arrow's trademark is his ability to improvise songs for the people he meets. He believes this ability is a gift and says that the lyrics just "come to him." Arrow performs at many hotel restaurants in Grenada's tourist belt, often accompanying himself on the guitar. When he is not performing, he tends his land in Requin in the parish of Saint David.

MUSICAL INSTRUMENTS

The most distinctive musical instrument in Grenada is the pan. Like calypso, the pan originated in Trinidad, and it is an instrument born out of ingenuity and creativity. People were determined to make music even when the colonial authorities banned their traditional percussion instruments. They found that the tops of discarded oil drums, which they retrieved from the garbage, could be coaxed into making music by "tuning" them, or beating them into shape.

The pan is the basic instrument of the steel band and is made from an oil drum with the bottom removed. The depth of the pan determines the pitch. After the bottom of the drum has been removed, the top is beaten into a concave shape divided into a number of sections separated by grooves that are chiseled into the surface. Each section is then beaten from the inside of the drum so that its surface is raised.

There are several types of pan: the ping-pong or soprano pan, the second or alto pan, the third or tenor pan, and the bass pan. Each pan is able to play the notes of the musical scale, and a good steel band can play a wide range of popular and classical music.

The steel pan is one of the most distinctive sounds of Grenada.

FOLK DANCES

Many of the Grenadian folk dances originated with the African slavery, such as the *bongo* (BON-goh) and the *kalinda* (KA-lihn-dah). Both dances were traditionally performed at wakes in the belief that they helped the dead person transit from this world to the next. While the *bongo* has graceful movements, the *kalinda* resembles a choreographed stick fight.

The French and the English also contributed to the dance heritage of Grenada. The quadrille, a French dance popular in 18th-century England, was introduced to Grenada by the English. The quadrille was traditionally accompanied by tambourine, bass drum, violin, and triangle. At the end of the dance, it was the tradition to throw a bouquet, with the next quadrille gathering held in the home of the person who caught it. Another French dance that arrived in Grenada via England was the lancers. It was performed by men dressed in tailcoats and frilled neckpieces and women in long flowing gowns.

The Africans developed the *belair*, a dance inspired by the quadrille and lancers. They performed this barefoot, and the women often wore bright headscarves with long-sleeve dresses and lacy petticoats, while the men had on headbands, colorful shirts, and white trousers or dungarees.

Grenadian traditional dancers performing at an event.

WARM CLIMATE, VIBRANT COLORS

The Grenadian hillside is covered with small, square houses that have been built on pier foundations. As there is no need to insulate against the cold, the outdoors is "brought into" the living environment in the form of verandas, porches, balconies, and large windows with louvered shutters. At first, houses retained the natural hues of their building materials, but when paint became readily available, islanders used it to express their creativity on the exterior of their homes.

There are no basements in the houses. A series of steps usually leads the visitor up to the main door. The houses have one or two stories, and there are no high-rise buildings. Grenada prides itself on the fact that no building is allowed to be taller than a coconut palm.

There are many interesting historical buildings with distinctly European, especially French and English, architecture. The wrought-iron work along the Esplanade and Market Square in Saint George's is an example of French influence. The British influence is seen in the Georgian-style buildings.

A fine example of a traditional, colorful house.

FOLK ARTISTS

The history of art is relatively young in Grenada. In the 20th century many Grenadians took up painting, drawing, and sculpting. Most artists were self-taught painters who used watercolors and oils. Instead of canvas, which is not easily available on the island, hardboard and other types of fiberboard were used as surfaces. Paintings include scenes of island life: blue skies, clear waters, fishermen and their nets, market bustle, and children at play.

One very well-known painter was Canute Caliste, who came from Carriacou. Known locally as CC or Old Head, he was eccentric and claimed to have been inspired as a child by a mermaid in Tyrrel Bay. After meeting her, he ran home to his mother, never went to school again, and didn't read or write, instead expressing himself through art and music. His paintings, described as "childlike" or "primitive," often featured mermaids in some way. He was also a self-taught fiddler who once played for Queen Elizabeth at Buckingham Palace. He died in 2005.

Renowned painter Canute Caliste with his wife and grandchild.

Grenadian artists are supported by the Grenada Arts Council, which organizes annual art shows. These shows provide many young artists an opportunity to exhibit their work outside of catering to the tourists' need for souvenirs. One young artist is Freddy Paul, who has become known in Grenada for his colorful and vibrant paintings. Paul is a watercolorist whose dream of having an art gallery has come true. He is self-taught and has won a number of awards.

GRENADIAN HANDICRAFTS

Grenadian handicrafts have a long history, beginning with the early settlers who arrived from South America. Excavations at Point Salines in the south of Grenada and at Duquesne Bay and Sauteurs in the north have unearthed finely crafted terra-cotta cooking pots and ceremonial vessels, intricate sculptures, arrowheads, and stone carvings.

Some handicrafts on display at the Grenadian National Institute of Handicrafts. The institute tries to keep these skills alive through its production and training center.

Today many craftspeople make batik material; weave straw, bamboo, and wicker into hats, bags, and purses; carve furniture, kitchen utensils, and other useful and decorative household items out of mahogany, red cedar, and other woods; and make articles out of coral and turtle shell.

The villagers of Marquis, on the eastern side of the main island, are known as expert weavers able to fashion all kinds of useful objects out of wild palm leaves.

THEATER AND LITERATURE

Grenadian theater began mainly as Shakespearean theater, a result of the English colonial period. Shakespearean plays were performed annually and on special occasions for the entertainment of the people. Many Grenadian actors got their start during this period. At the same time, there was theater based on folklore.

The public library in Saint George's was formerly a warehouse.

In the 1960s and 1970s Grenadian playwrights became more inward looking and began to produce West Indian plays. Writers searched for a cultural identity, and oral poets performed in front of large crowds. Wilfred Redhead is an author from this period whose plays have been published and performed all over the Caribbean. His book *A City on a Hill* is a memoir of life in Saint George's.

Grenadian writer Omowale David Franklyn's book *Bridging the Two Grenadas* looks at the formation and transformation of Grenadian society and in particular the influence of two former prime ministers, Eric Gairy and Maurice Bishop.

Writer and academician Merle Collins has published several books. Her first collection of poetry, *Because the Dawn Breaks*, was published when she was a member of African Dawn, a group that performed poetry and mime to African music.

LEISURE

Youths playing cricket on the beach.

Cricket and soccer are two of the most popular sports in Grenada.

THE BRITISH NOT ONLY LEFT Grenadians a legacy in their government, court, and education systems, but they also shared their love of soccer and cricket. Other leisure activities revolve around water, which is not surprising, since Grenada is surrounded by water and has a tropical climate.

Grenadians love to have picnics by the sea or waterfalls and to hike through the beautiful mountain ranges in the center of the island. Hunting is also popular.

Simple pleasures such as circle games continue to be passed down from generation to generation. Modern pastimes such as watching television have also pervaded the Grenadian lifestyle. With the growth of tourism, nightclubs have become a part of island life, and many residents now prefer to dance the night away.

CRICKET

Cricket was introduced to the English-speaking Caribbean region by the British, and Grenadians are excellent players. Cricket is played on an open green with two teams of 11 players each. The teams, whose

Right: A young, aspiring musician with his homemade guitar.

Young Grenadians playing cricket. The rules of cricket are complex, and a match may last for several days.

players traditionally wear predominantly white uniforms, take turns trying to bat the ball and hit the wicket of the opposing team.

Unfortunately, with their small populations, individual island nations have difficulty producing enough excellent players to form national teams that can compete internationally. Grenadian cricketers vie with players from among other English-speaking Caribbean countries in competitions to select the best players to represent the West Indies in international championship games. Excitement runs particularly high when the West Indies plays against England.

Junior Murray was lauded as Grenada's best cricket player during his career. He made sporting history when he became the first Grenadian to represent the West Indies in an international championship game. He has since retired. More recent Grenadian cricketers of note are Devon Smith, Andre Fletcher, and Rawl Lewis.

SOCCER

English football, or soccer, is another popular sport in Grenada. The Grenada Football Association has 35 member clubs that compete each year in the premier league. English football is played by two teams of 11 players each. A game lasts for 90 minutes, and the objective is for the teams to score as many goals as possible.

Grenada's national football team, splashy in their green, yellow, and red uniforms, is affectionately known as the Spice Boyz. The most successful football club is probably the Hurricanes. It has won the Grenada National Championship more often than any other club, winning every year from 1969 to 1976. Jason Roberts, born in England to a Grenadian father and a Guyanese mother, has been called Grenada's most famous footballer. Although his home club is in Blackburn, England, he has played for Grenada in world football events. Shalrie Joseph, who plays for an American club, was named Grenada's Footballer of the Year in 2003.

Two local teams having a friendly soccer match.

Every boys' school has cricket and football teams, and it is common to see young boys kicking a ball around on any available open ground. The 15,000-seat National Stadium, built in 2000 at a cost of $23 million, provides a prestigious venue for all major football and cricket games and field and track events on the island. It hosted the International Cricket Council (ICC) World Cup matches of 2007.

Scuba enthusiasts loading up the boat for a dive.

WATER SPORTS

There are numerous sailing events throughout the year, many hosted by the Grenada Yacht Club. They attract participants from all over the world. Every Easter the Grenada Yacht Club holds a regatta where the main attraction is a race from Trinidad to Grenada. The Carriacou Regatta, which is held during a weekend in late July or early August, is a much bigger and older affair. It began in 1965 as a local boat race using traditional fishing boats and has evolved into a major Caribbean event, with keen competition among local sailors and those from neighboring islands.

Fishing, scuba diving, and snorkeling are other popular sports. There is good game fishing for marlin, sailfish, and yellowfin tuna. Anglers from all over the world, but especially from the United States and other Caribbean islands, compete in the Spice Island Billfish Tournament, which is held every January.

Grenada has some of the most beautiful beaches in the world. It is possible to wade into the sea and watch schools of fish in the clear blue waters. Even in the Carenage, an area where ships arrive every day to unload cargo, one can spot colorful reef fish. Coral reefs abound off the north, east, and south coasts of Grenada, off the east coasts of Carriacou and Petite Martinique, and around the smaller islands of the Grenadines. It is no wonder that these islands attract many snorkelers and divers.

OTHER LEISURE ACTIVITIES

On weekends families often enjoy a picnic by the sea, a river, or a waterfall. Grenada has several lovely waterfalls: the Concord and Annandale falls in the parish of Saint John, Tufton Hall Waterfall in Saint Mark, and Saint Margaret Falls in the heart of the Grand Etang National Park.

A traditional Grenadian picnic is a simple affair. Almost everything that is required for a meal is available on the spot. Three stones form a triangle on which a pot is put, dry twigs and branches are placed underneath, and a fire is lit. Bowls, hollowed out of calabash shells, are the only containers needed, and a spoon is quickly fashioned out of a twig.

A group of friends playing on the beach.

A little boy playing with his toy yacht.

Hiking is another activity accessible to all. The central mountains, especially those in the Grand Etang National Park, have many well-developed nature trails. Mount Qua Qua provides the hiker with a wonderful view of the surrounding countryside. Some people love to hunt. They shoot monkeys and armadillos. Some consider the meat of these animals a delicacy.

CHILDREN'S GAMES

Circle games were popular in the past. Two well-known examples of circle games that have come to us from the Caribbean are Brown Girl in the Ring and Here We Go Loop-de-Lou. These song games were played in schoolyards, at home with friends, or with parents and elders who taught the art of singing to the young.

In Carriacou similar songs called pass plays were sung by a circle of adults, most notably at wakes. Another is a *kalinda*, or stick-fighting, song. The stickman and his supporters sing a challenge to all to "meet me on the road."

Today children spend their time cycling with friends, playing soccer and basketball, or pitching marbles. Girls enjoy jumping rope and playing jacks, baseball, and hopscotch. A popular game called *morual* (MOR-u-al) involves drawing a rectangle in the dirt and dividing it into 8 or 10 sections. A ball is thrown, and the players move through the sections and try to gain control of as many as possible.

Some families gather in the living room to relax and watch television. If a home is without a television set, time is spent reading a book or talking and relaxing with friends under the shade of a large tree.

RELAXING WITH RUM

Men like to get together with their friends at the local rum shop for a "happy hour" of "eights" and a game of dominoes or cards. An "eight" is a measure of rum that is often drunk in one gulp or consumed a little more slowly and shared among friends. If one desires, the rum can be washed down with a glass of iced water. Dominoes is a game that is taken seriously in Grenada. Men form clubs that compete in a championship.

NIGHTLIFE

Nightlife in Grenada is picking up due to the increasing emphasis on tourism. Most hotels and resorts have their own clubs catering to tourists and locals alike. These places offer live entertainment with dancing, drumming, and steel bands. The music is "hot," and the steel bands play soca, reggae, and other Caribbean music. Besides catering to the needs of the local population, these places offer tourists a cultural cabaret, a chance to sample a little of the local culture and folklore.

The town of Saint George's is rather quiet in the evenings. There are two movie houses, the Reno and the Triple Reels.

FOLKTALES

Storytelling is a very important tradition in Grenada that springs from African roots. Folktales are a means of teaching people about their past, their culture, and the values of their society.

Story time often begins with someone calling out "Tim tim" or "Crick crack," to which the children respond with "Papa welcome" or whatever the local custom happens to be. Then everyone gathers around to listen to famous stories about Anansi. Half-man, half-spider, Anansi is cunning, greedy, and shrewd.

In the Anansi stories, small and seemingly weak animals are able to overcome strong and threatening ones such as tigers and pythons by their wit and trickery. It is customary for the storyteller to finish by announcing, "The story end and wire bend." The children are then treated to some food or drink. The Anansi stories come from the days of slavery, when the art of storytelling brought great comfort to an oppressed people.

FESTIVALS

Young women participating in a parade
during a Grenadian festival.

G RENADA HAS MANY FESTIVALS and holidays, but perhaps the most important and best-known occasion is Carnival. This is Grenada's annual national festival. Grenada shares this celebration with many other countries in the region, especially those with a Roman Catholic tradition, such as Brazil and most of the other islands in the Caribbean.

As the majority of Grenadians are Roman Catholic, feast days in the Church calendar are also festival days. Many of these are movable feasts— that is, the calendar day on which it falls changes from year to year.

Grenadian festivities are marked by great feasting and drinking, laughter, music, and dancing that last throughout the day.

CARNIVAL

Historically Carnival allowed people to have a big celebration before Lent, when they

Carnival is one of Grenada's most celebrated and colorful festivals.

Right: Flags in the national colors decorate the streets of Saint George's during Independence Day.

A local group, the Grand Anse Beach Pierrots, performing during Carnival.

were required to fast. Carnival was their last chance to dance, sing, and make merry before the 40 days of the Lenten season.

When Grenada was a French colony, the planters celebrated this time with much socializing. They had dinners and concerts and paraded in beautiful costumes. After emancipation in 1834, former slaves used Carnival as a vehicle to parody the planters. The masked players imitated estate owners and other important people, the use of disguise enabling them to step over the boundaries of color and social class.

Carnival has evolved during the years. The costumes and masquerades have been retained, but the mood is mainly celebratory. There are talent contests, steel-band performances, parades, and a search for the year's Calypso King and Carnival Queen. Grenada celebrates Carnival on the Monday and Tuesday of the second week of August, although the preparations begin long before then. The party continues late into the evening.

Carnival has retained a little more of its old flavor on Carriacou. In the past, Pierrots, or clowns with white faces, in each village would gather months before Carnival and challenge each other in wrestling and reciting Shakespeare. From these contests would come kings from each village who would all meet on Shrove Tuesday. Today this riotous celebration has been tamed into a contest among participants who dress as Pierrots, in long socks, lace skirts, and long-sleeve shirts, to recite from Shakespeare's *Julius Caesar*.

PLAYING MAS

A big part of Carnival is dressing up in costumes and masks, or "playing mas," as Grenadians call it. Many of these costumes and characters have historic significance. The night before Carnival is traditionally devoted to mocking and driving out devils. Many of the masqueraders dress as jab-jab (JAB-jab), which is a creole word for "devil." They use body paint, grease, or molasses to color their bodies, and they dance in a pantomime that tells of their escape from hell to heaven. Sometimes the Carnival revelers dress to parody events of the past year.

Another traditional Carnival character is Pierrot, a clownlike entertainer with a white face who usually wears a loose, fancy white dress. This dates back to a time when itinerant minstrels would whiten their faces and wear long white dresses. Related to Pierrot is Short Knee. When former slaves were allowed to take part in the celebrations, they imitated the Pierrot character. They would travel from village to village challenging others in oratory. But beneath their long dresses, they hid weapons that they used when brawls broke out. When these long costumes were outlawed by the government, revelers took to wearing baggy pants that reached just below the knee, hence the name "Short Knee."

The largest celebration of Fisherman's Birthday is held in the village of Gouyave.

FEAST DAYS

Movable feasts are festival days that change from year to year depending on the liturgical calendar. Corpus Christi occurs eight weeks after Easter. It is celebrated with a special church service and street processions. Although it is a Roman Catholic festival, other churches join in the celebrations in a spirit of unity and ecumenism. This is reciprocated when the Anglican community celebrates the feast of Saint George. Christians from the other churches join in the procession through the town of Saint George's.

The Feast of Saint Peter and Saint Paul on June 29 is reason for another big celebration. It is called Fisherman's Birthday because Saint Peter was a fisherman. Grenadians celebrate this festival because many of them come from fishing families.

Girls singing Christmas carols.

Christmas was once celebrated with a traditional maypole dance. Young girls, each holding one end of a ribbon that was attached to the pole, would dance around it, weaving in and out to create patterns with their ribbons. Dancing the maypole is no longer performed, but Christmas is still a very special time of the year. Houses are thoroughly cleaned, new things replace the old, and everybody dresses in his or her best clothes to go visiting. Musicians go around caroling or serenading. Kitchens bustle with the enormous amount of cooking that needs to be done to ensure that anyone who passes by or steps in the door is feted to his heart's content.

PARANG

Parang, a festival that occurs the weekend before Christmas, is unique to Carriacou. Parang came to Grenada from South America via Trinidad. It grew out of the tradition of going from house to house caroling. Today it is less a celebration of Christmas and has an identity of its own.

Parang songs are sung in English. Full of humor, the songs are often impromptu and tell of someone's misdeeds. The festival was started in 1977 by the Mount Royal Progressive Youth Movement, a nonprofit organization that wanted to celebrate this aspect of the island's culture.

The three-day festival begins with a Hosanna Bands contest—a carol-singing contest among village groups. This is followed by a calypso and soca jam session. Performers from Carriacou and other parts of Grenada entertain a large crowd, and foreign artistes are usually invited. Festivities reach a climax on the third night when Parang groups compete for the challenge trophy and other prizes. Traditional Carriacou dances such as the quadrille add to the festivities.

BIG DRUM

Carriacou is particularly known for Big Drum. The festival is experiencing a revival, especially as young Carriacouans are renewing their interest in their heritage of African drumming and dances.

Big Drum music uses three drums. The center drum is called the cot drum; the two side drums are bula drums. Dancers and singers accompany the drums. The lead singer sings parables of repression, warfare, and other troubles or tales of gossip. Some songs tell of a longing for West Africa, while others lament the lives of the people or ridicule the oppressors. Dancers are called forth by the beat of the drum, and

Steel-band musicians preparing for a performance.

they dance in a circle. The dances reflect the African heritage of the various peoples who came to the island—the Kromanti, the Ibo, the Mandingo, the Chamba, the Banda, the Moko, and others. The Kromanti dance is the most significant because the Kromanti, originally from Ghana, were one of the first groups to come to Carriacou. Every ceremony opens and closes with the Kromanti dance.

MAROON

Associated with the Big Drum is Maroon, an especially big sacrificial feast. Each year for the Dumfries Maroon in Carriacou several families, often related, will prepare food that is put on trays and then placed on both sides of the road leading to Dumfries. Some food is taken from each tray by specially appointed people and presented to the Big Drum participants who will perform in the evening. The rest of the food is offered to passersby.

BOAT-LAUNCHING FESTIVAL

Boatbuilding has a long and important history on Carriacou, so there is a celebration when a new boat is to be launched. The ceremony begins with a Big Drum performance and a *saraca*, followed by the pouring of spirits and the sprinkling of rice around the boat. Animals are ritually slaughtered. Chickens are killed in the galley to symbolize an abundance of food, a ram is killed on the stern to bless the ship with fair winds, and a sheep is slaughtered over the bow to make steering easy. A second round of spirits is then poured around the boat.

A priest is usually invited to bless the boat. He says his prayers and sprinkles holy water over the boat while accompanied by two people who represent the godparents of the boat. The culmination of the ceremony is the unfurling of a flag with the boat's name. Then, as the drums roll, there is the important "cutting down" of the boat. Men all along the side of the boat use axes to cut the posts on which it rests, and the boat is gradually lowered into the sea.

Bands playing only percussion instruments sing about political and other talked-about events of the year. If one does something scandalous, especially close to the month of December, one might be warned to "be careful, we go put you on the banjo!" Most songs are sung with a biting humor. Names are sometimes linked with the rumors sung in the Parang songs. This has led to threats of legal suits against the singers.

Spices for sale. Spices are an important element of Grenadian cuisine.

THE CARIBBEAN IS A MEETING PLACE for many cuisines, including African, Spanish, British, Dutch, French, Portuguese, Chinese, and East Indian. Grenadians have been able to match this rich heritage with a plentiful variety of fresh foods for the cooking pot. Add spices—for Grenada is known as the Isle of Spice— and the result is a cuisine that is varied, interesting, and unique to the country.

Slavery has left an important imprint on the country's cooking. The slaves, rooted in poverty, could not afford meat or fish. Instead they

Grenadians doing their grocery shopping at the Saint George's open-air market.

Grenadian cuisine is influenced by many cultures. Most Grenadians buy their groceries at open-air markets. Spices are an integral part of Grenadian cooking; meat is often marinated in a variety of spices before being cooked. Besides rice and roti, tubers and roots such as yams and cassavas are staples in the Grenadian diet. Fresh fruit juice is also very popular.

**A variety of
bananas for sale.**

resorted to cooking with "ground provisions"—starchy root vegetables such as yams, dasheens, and sweet potatoes. Beans, salt fish, and salt pork added some variety to their diet. Ground provisions remain an important part of the diet today.

GROUND PROVISIONS

While the potato is a staple food in Grenadian cooking, ground provisions are a popular substitute. Dasheens, tannias, eddoes, yams, cassavas, and sweet potatoes may be steamed, boiled, or added to stews. There are also two members of the banana family that are equally versatile—the plantain, which looks like a large green banana, and the bluggoe, which is shorter and thicker in size. These rather starchy, solid, and bland fruits are often fried and eaten as a snack.

Another starchy item that often makes its appearance on the dinner table is breadfruit. This round, green fruit is cooked and eaten like a vegetable. Breadfruit is native to the Pacific Islands, and the story is that it was introduced in the late 18th century by Captain Bligh of *Mutiny on the Bounty* infamy to provide food for the slaves. It is bland and chewy, but it absorbs the flavors of the spices with which it is cooked. Breadfruit balls are made by mashing the breadfruit, forming it into balls, and deep-frying them. Breadfruit soup is made with salted meat and onions. Grenada's national dish, oil down, is made with breadfruit and meat, usually chicken or pork, cooked in coconut milk. A kind of heavy dumpling is added to the stew. Turmeric produces the characteristic yellow color of the dish.

ROTI AND RICE

When the Europeans arrived, they introduced new foods—wine, olive oil, cheese, salami, and European spices. They also brought bread. Slaves were taught by their planter families to make bread, but being used to ground provisions they made a heavier kind of bread. Today bread is found in many forms but most commonly as a kind of long roll or "French" bread, with a crusty surface. Bakeries also make buns and butter bread—French rolls made of a heavy, unleavened dough—as well as a lighter version leavened with yeast. People drop by the bakeries during the day to buy not only bread but also drinks and "pies," which are squares or triangles of pastry filled with meat, fish, salami, cheese, or jam.

After slavery was abolished, new groups of indentured laborers arrived in the region and brought with them more new foods. The East Indians introduced curry powder and a thin pancake made of flour and water, called a roti. The Chinese brought Asian spices and vegetables.

Grenadians have transformed the Indian roti and curry into something of their own. The pancake is made into a wrap and filled with a curry-flavored potato-and-meat mixture that is a meal in itself.

Rice, which was probably introduced by the East Indian and Chinese communities, is also popular. It is often cooked with pigeon peas, also called yellow peas. Alternatively, rice is cooked with spices and is then known as seasoning rice. Pigeon peas may also be served on their own as a side dish or cooked with salt beef and other meats and seasonings.

ISLE OF SPICE

No discussion of Grenadian food can be complete without mentioning spices. The island is known as the Isle of Spice for good reason. All kinds are grown here: cloves, cinnamon, ginger, vanilla, bay, turmeric (which Grenadians call saffron), pimento, pepper, nutmeg, and mace. These are used in many combinations to flavor all sorts of meat dishes, cakes, and sweets.

Chicken, pork, beef, and mutton are all part of the Grenadian diet. These are marinated with spices and cooked slowly. Marinating and seasoning are

The distinctive flavor of Grenadian food comes from the coconut oil in which most of the food is cooked. When one wanders through the markets, it is common to be approached by young boys selling bottles of coconut oil for cooking.

Baskets of red mace and nutmeg.

important elements in Grenadian cooking. Except for tender cuts of meat and quick-cooking foods such as fish, hardly anything is cooked without being properly seasoned and marinated for a few hours. The secret of spicing the food is to ensure that the taste of the individual spices do not stand out; rather the spices should combine to produce a subtle blend of flavors.

THE PEPPER POT

Grenadians cook lots of soups and stews. The "one pot," a combination of vegetables, meat, and often seafood, makes a popular holiday lunch. A soup commonly found in restaurants is the thick, dark green callaloo soup. The callaloo is the tender leaf of the dasheen plant, and it looks and tastes like spinach. It is simmered in coconut milk and spices until soft.

The pepper pot is a special stew that can contain several kinds of meat. The most important ingredient is cassareep, which is made from the cassava plant and acts as a preservative. It gives the stew a distinctive bittersweet

The West Indies believes that it produces the world's hottest pepper, the Scotch bonnet. However, it is facing competition from the bhut jolokia, which comes from India. But even if it has been toppled from the topmost rung of the fire ladder, the Scotch bonnet is a pepper to be treated with great respect. It is many times hotter than the jalapeño and the serrano, two peppers commonly found in North American stores. Its name comes from the crinkled crown of the pepper, which some believe looks like a traditional Scottish bonnet. There are red, yellow, orange, and green ones. The hottest part of the pepper is not the seeds, as some people believe, but the white veins, which contain the capsaicin that is responsible for the fiery power of the vegetable.

It is difficult to understand what it is that makes the heat of the pepper such an attraction for people who live in hot countries. One theory is that it fosters perspiration, which is the body's natural cooling mechanism. Another is that there is a "high" that comes from eating hot peppers that makes those who love it want more. The body reacts to the pain caused by eating the peppers by producing endorphins, the same natural compounds that produce the so-called runner's high.

Early European explorers found that if sailors ate peppers during long sea voyages, they did not suffer from scurvy. Peppers are rich in vitamins A and C.

A drinks menu at a restaurant in Grenada.

taste. The pepper pot can last indefinitely, as the cook keeps replenishing it with more meat and vegetables as they are consumed. Some pepper pots have been kept for more than 20 years.

Souse is a festive dish made with pig's feet. The feet are cleaned and boiled until tender. The meat is then sliced and combined with a sauce made from garlic, onions, lime juice, salt, and pepper. Seafood is often served for dinner. Conch, or *lambi* (LAM-bi), is the most popular seafood delicacy.

Grenadian food, though well spiced and seasoned, is seldom chili-hot although the Caribbean is home to one of the world's hottest peppers, the Scotch bonnet. But nearly every restaurant table will have a bottle of hot sauce on it.

REFRESHING DRINKS

Fruit juices abound in Grenada: mango, papaya, golden apple (called June plum in other parts of the Caribbean), orange, avocado, guava, passion fruit, lime, banana, five-finger fruit (also known as carambola or starfruit), soursop, and sweetsop (or custard apple), to name a few.

Grenadians make juice with the most unlikely of ingredients. Even the sour tamarind is made into a deliciously tart drink. Ginger beer, which is nonalcoholic, is also extremely popular. Mawby is made by boiling pieces of a tree native to the Caribbean together with some orange peel and spices. This produces a dark bitter liquid that is diluted, sweetened, and left to ferment for a few days. The resulting drink is reminiscent of licorice, leaving a lingering and slightly bitter, herbal aftertaste. Sea moss is a milky sweet drink made from seaweed.

Sorrel is drunk during the Christmas season. It is made from the fleshy dark-red sepals of a small plant from the hibiscus family that is also native to the Caribbean. The sepals are picked and soaked in water with bay leaves, cloves, and cinnamon, and then they are strained to make a dark-colored drink. The plant flowers only around December.

A common scene in the markets is that of vendors slashing off the tops of coconuts. Coconut juice is popular with shoppers who, after some hours of shopping under the blazing sun, like to enjoy this cooling drink in the shade.

RUM

Rum is the alcoholic drink that is most associated with the Caribbean. Rum is produced from sugarcane, and there are as many kinds of rum as there are islands in the region. There are several rum distilleries on Grenada Island.

The Rivers Rum Distillery (formerly called the River Antoine Rum Distillery) was started in 1785, making it the oldest distillery still in operation in the Caribbean. Sadly, the Dunfermline Rum Distillery in Saint Andrew, which was built in 1797, closed its doors in 2007. Clarke's Court is a large Grenadian distillery that produces many sugarcane-based products such as high-quality rum, spiced rum, and spice liquor. Two other distilleries are the Grenada Sugar Factory and Westerhall Rum Distillery.

The color of rum ranges from almost colorless to a dark brown. A light-colored rum is aged in ordinary oak casks, while a darker rum is aged in charred-oak casks. Sugar caramel is sometimes added for color. Rum is also used in cooking, baking, and many cocktail concoctions. One concoction is rum punch, a drink that can be traced back to plantation days.

No mention of rum on Grenada is complete without mentioning Jack Iron, a rum so high in alcohol that if you put ice cubes in a glass of it, they will sink to the bottom! This drink is most associated with Carriacou, where it is the island's special drink.

SPICY CHICKEN WINGS

Spicy grilled chicken wings is a must item at any Caribbean-themed barbeque (in Jamaica, they call it jerk chicken), and this recipe is made particularly Grenadian by the addition of hot-pepper seasoning and nutmeg.

Marinade

1 onion, chopped	½ teaspoon (2.5 ml) ground cinnamon
2 garlic cloves, minced	¼ cup (60 ml) finely chopped jalapeño peppers
½ teaspoon (2.5 ml) dried thyme	several dashes of hot sauce, such as Tabasco, to taste
1 teaspoon (5 ml) ground ginger	2 tablespoons (30 ml) soy sauce
¼ teaspoon (1.25 ml) grated nutmeg	¼ cup (60 ml) vegetable oil

Combine these ingredients in a food processor and puree until they are well mixed. Take about 18 chicken wings with their tips cut off. Put the wings in a large bowl and pour the marinade in, making sure that it is well rubbed into the wings. Allow the chicken to marinade overnight in the refrigerator. To cook in an oven, preheat the oven to 450°F (232°C), and bake the wings for 30 minutes or longer, till they are properly cooked. Turn the wings over at least once during the cooking to ensure that they are browned on both sides. If you are grilling the wings, place them in one layer on the rack and grill over high heat for about 15 minutes or until the wings are properly cooked. Turn frequently to avoid burning.

GINGER BEER

Ginger beer used to be given to slaves on the estates so that they could celebrate with a nonalcoholic drink. It is a popular drink in Grenada during Christmas and is served in most restaurants.

¼ pound (550 g) ginger root

1 lime or lemon

3 cloves

5 cups (1.25 L) water

Remove the brown skin of the ginger root and slice the root thinly. Add the juice of one lime or lemon, three cloves, and five cups of water. Bring it all to a boil for about five minutes so that the ginger flavor is extracted. Allow it to stand overnight, then strain the liquid and sweeten it to taste. Pour into a glass bottle and leave it for a few days until a little foam forms on the surface. When this happens, your ginger beer is ready to drink. Refrigerate it or serve it cold on ice for a wonderfully gingery, sweet, and refreshing summer drink.

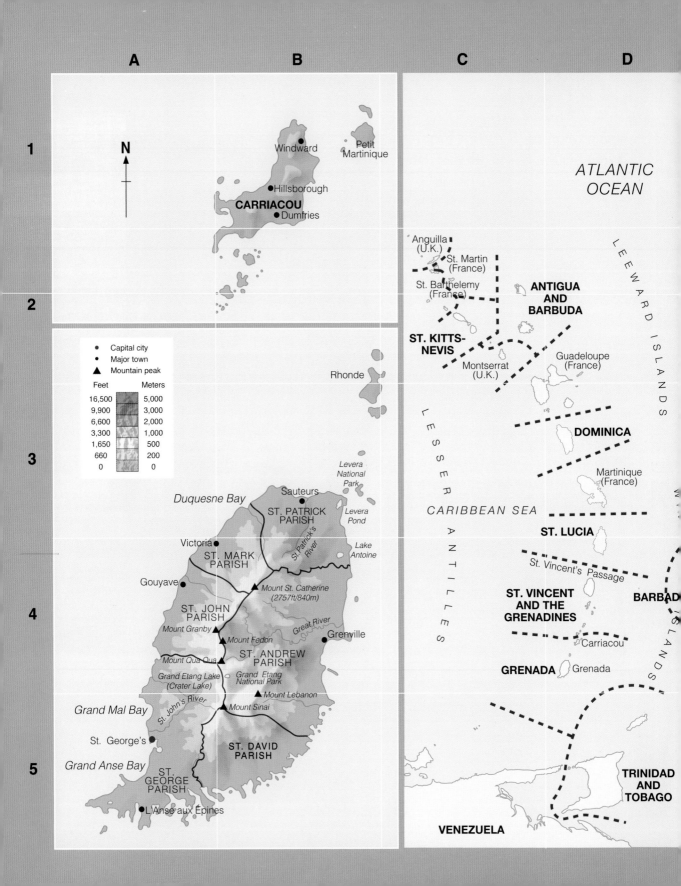

A　　　**B**　　　**C**　　　**D**

1

N

Windward

Petit
Martinique

Hillsborough

CARRIACOU

Dumfries

*ATLANTIC
OCEAN*

Anguilla ■
(U.K.)
St. Martin
(France)

St. Barthelemy
(France)

**ANTIGUA
AND
BARBUDA**

L E E W A R D

**ST. KITTS-
NEVIS**

Montserrat
(U.K.)

Guadeloupe
(France)

I S L A N D S

2

- ● Capital city
- ● Major town
- ▲ Mountain peak

Feet	Meters
16,500	5,000
9,900	3,000
6,600	2,000
3,300	1,000
1,650	500
660	200
0	0

Rhonde

L E S S E R

DOMINICA

Martinique
(France)

A N T I L L E S

CARIBBEAN SEA

ST. LUCIA

3

Duquesne Bay

Sauteurs

**ST. PATRICK
PARISH**

*Levera
National
Park*

*Levera
Pond*

Victoria ●

**ST. MARK
PARISH**

*St. Patrick's
River*

*Lake
Antoine*

St. Vincent's Passage

**ST. VINCENT
AND THE
GRENADINES**

BARBAD

4

Gouyave ●

**ST. JOHN
PARISH**

▲ Mount St. Catherine
(2757ft/840m)

Mount Granby ▲

▲ Mount Fedon

Great River

Grenville ●

Carriacou

Mount Qua Qua ▲

**ST. ANDREW
PARISH**

GRENADA ◯ Grenada

I S L A N D S

*Grand Etang Lake
(Crater Lake)*

◯ *Grand Etang
National Park*

Grand Mal Bay

St. John's River

▲ Mount Lebanon

▲ Mount Sinai

St. George's ●

**ST. DAVID
PARISH**

5

Grand Anse Bay

**ST.
GEORGE
PARISH**

**TRINIDAD
AND
TOBAGO**

● L'Anse aux Épines

VENEZUELA

MAP OF GRENADA

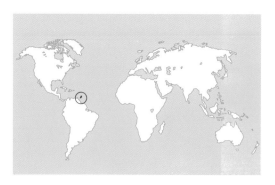

ECONOMIC GRENADA

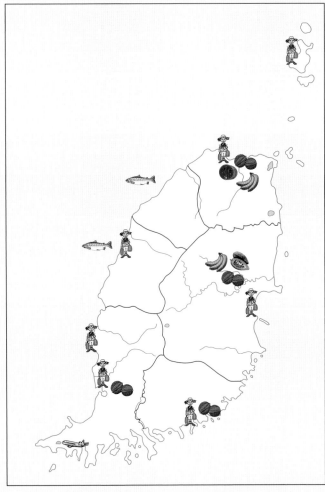

Services

 Airport

 Tourism

Agriculture

 Bananas

 Cocoa

 Nutmeg

Manufacturing

 Rum distilling

Natural Resources

 Fishing

ABOUT THE ECONOMY

OVERVIEW

Historically, the agricultural sector was the biggest earner for Grenada's economy. All that changed when Hurricane Ivan damaged almost 90 percent of Grenada's agricultural land and crop in 2004. This sector is only just beginning to recover. However, the country produces about a third of the world's nutmeg, and its spice exports are an important component of the economy. Tourism now accounts for 76 percent of Grenada's GDP. Small industries such as garment and furniture making, food processing, and rum distillation also help to boost the economy.

GROSS DOMESTIC PRODUCT (GDP)

$1.156 billion (2009 estimate)

EMPLOYMENT PROFILE BY OCCUPATION

62 percent in service industry, 24 percent in agriculture, 14 percent in industry

UNEMPLOYMENT RATE

12.5 percent (2000 estimate)

CURRENCY

1 East Caribbean dollar (XCD) = 100 cents
US$1 = 2.7 XCD (November 2010)

MAJOR IMPORTS

Food, manufactured goods, machinery, fuel, and chemicals

MAJOR EXPORTS

Bananas, cocoa, spices, fruit, fish, vegetables, clothing, and flour

INFLATION RATE

3.7 percent (2007 estimate)

POPULATION BELOW POVERTY LINE

32 percent (2000)

POINTS OF ENTRY

Airports: Lauriston Airport (Carriacou) and Maurice Bishop International Airport (Grenada Island)
Port: Port of Saint George's

LAND TRANSPORTATION

Total road network: 700 miles (1,127 km); 427 miles (687 km) paved and 273 miles (440 km) unpaved (2000)

MAJOR INDUSTRIES

Food and beverages, textiles, light assembly operations, tourism, and construction

INTERNET

Country code: gd; 24,000 Internet users (2008 estimate)

CULTURAL GRENADA

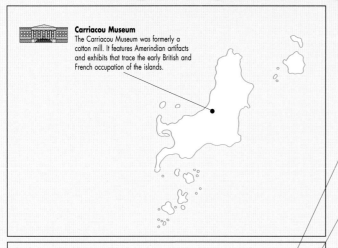

Carriacou Museum
The Carriacou Museum was formerly a cotton mill. It features Amerindian artifacts and exhibits that trace the early British and French occupation of the islands.

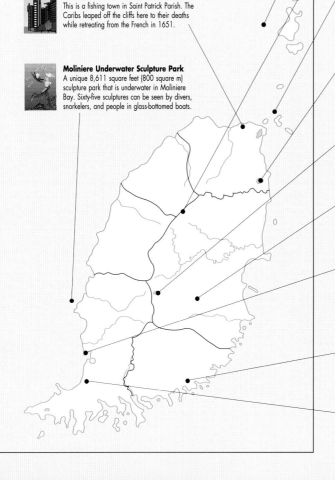

Sauteurs
This is a fishing town in Saint Patrick Parish. The Caribs leaped off the cliffs here to their deaths while retreating from the French in 1651.

Moliniere Underwater Sculpture Park
A unique 8,611 square feet (800 square m) sculpture park that is underwater in Moliniere Bay. Sixty-five sculptures can be seen by divers, snorkelers, and people in glass-bottomed boats.

Volcano Kick-'em-Jenny
An active submarine volcano that rises 4,265 feet (1,300 m) above the sea floor. The first record of an eruption from this volcano was in 1939. Since then, the volcano has erupted on at least 12 occasions.

Mount Saint Catherine
At 2,757 feet (840 m) high, this is the highest point in Grenada. It has a horseshoe-shaped crater open to the east with several lava domes in it. It is not known when its last eruption happened.

Levera National Park
This national park has a saltwater lagoon with a white-sand beach sheltered by coral reefs with mangrove swamps on either side. This park is a haven for many bird species such as herons, black-necked stilts, common snipes, and other waterfowl. The beaches are a hatchery for sea turtles.

Lake Antoine
A shallow crater lake 20 feet (6 m) above sea level, 16 acres (6.5 ha) in size, it was formed 12,000 to 1,000 years ago during Grenada's final stage of volcanic activity. You can see many birds here, including the snail kite, the fulvous whistling duck, the gray kingbird, and the large-billed seed-finch.

Grand Etang Lake
This lake is 1,740 feet (530 m) above sea level, surrounded by a national park and forest reserve.

Grand Etang National Park
This is a popular area for hiking and birding. Its forests, ranging from lush rain forests to elfin woodlands, shelter many species of birds, including the broad-winged hawk, purple-throated carib, and Antillean crested hummingbird. In addition, it is home to mona monkeys, mongooses, armadillos, and opossums.

Grenada National Museum
On display here is an interesting collection of artifacts to do with the island's history and culture. It is housed in a historic old army barracks and prison buildings built in 1704.

La Sagesse Bay
La Sagesse Bay is a mangrove estuary that is one of the best bird-watching areas, attracting many bird species including the brown-crested flycatcher, Caribbean coot, and herons. It has fine beaches and offshore coral reefs for snorkeling.

Grand Anse Beach
This gorgeous beach boasts 2 miles (3.2 m) of beautiful fine white sand close to Saint George's, making it popular with locals and tourists.

ABOUT THE CULTURE

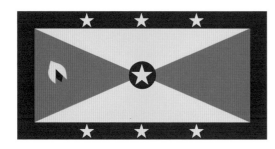

OFFICIAL NAME
Grenada

CAPITAL
Saint George's

LAND AREA
140 square miles (363 square km)

COASTLINE
75 miles (121 km)

ADMINISTRATIVE DIVISIONS
Six parishes—Saint Andrew, Saint David, Saint George, Saint John, Saint Mark, and Saint Patrick—and the dependencies of Carriacou and Petite Martinique

ANTHEM
"Hail Grenada"

OFFICIAL LANGUAGE
English

NATIONAL MOTTO
"Ever conscious of God, we aspire, build, and advance as one people"

NATIONAL BIRD
The Grenada dove

NATIONAL FLOWER
Bougainvillea

POPULATION
108,132 (2008 estimate)

ETHNIC GROUPS
Mainly people of African, East Indian, and European descent, with the largest proportion of the population, approximately 75 percent, of African descent

MAJOR RELIGIONS
Roman Catholic (53 percent), Anglican (13.8 percent), and other Protestant groups (33.2 percent)

LIFE EXPECTANCY
65.95 years

TIME ZONE
Grenada is in the Atlantic Standard Time Zone, one hour ahead of Eastern Standard Time and four hours behind Greenwich Mean Time

LITERACY RATE
96 percent

LEADERS IN GOVERNMENT
Eric Gairy (1922—97), named Grenada's first national hero in 2008; Maurice Bishop (1944—83); Herbert Blaize (1918—89); Keith Mitchell (b. 1946); and Tillman Thomas (b. 1947)

TIME LINE

IN GRENADA	IN THE WORLD
	753 B.C. Rome is founded.
8–1 B.C. Ciboneys settle in Grenada.	
A.D. 1–1000 Arawaks make Grenada their home.	**A.D. 600** Height of the Mayan civilization
A.D. 1000–1650 Caribs live on Grenada.	**1000** The Chinese perfect gunpowder and begin to use it in warfare.
1498 Columbus sets sight on Grenada.	**1530** Beginning of transatlantic slave trade organized by the Portuguese in Africa
1609 First attempted settlement by British merchants	
1638 French try to establish a settlement on Grenada.	
1650 Jacques-Dyel du Parquet, French governor of Martinique, purchases Grenada Island and establishes a settlement.	
1651–52 French wage war against the Caribs.	
1763 France cedes Grenada to the British as part of the Treaty of Paris.	
1779 French recapture Grenada.	
1783 Grenada restored to British rule in accordance with the Treaty of Versailles	
1791 Completion of forts at Richmond Hill and establishment of Market Square	
1795 Abortive rebellion by African planter Julien Fedon.	
1834 Emancipation; slavery is abolished.	

IN GRENADA	IN THE WORLD
	1869 The Suez Canal is opened.
	1914 World War I begins.
	1939 World War II begins.
	1945 The United States drops atomic bombs on Hiroshima and Nagasaki, Japan. World War II ends.
1958 Grenada becomes part of the Federation of the West Indies.	
1967 Grenada becomes autonomous, with foreign and defense affairs remaining under British control.	
1974 Grenada gains independence.	
1979 Prime Minster Eric Gairy ousted in a coup; People's Revolutionary Government under Maurice Bishop takes over.	
1983 Bishop is executed; coup sparks U.S. invasion of Grenada.	
1984 Return to elected government under Herbert Blaize	**1991** Breakup of the Soviet Union
	1997 Hong Kong is returned to China.
	2001 Terrorists crash planes in New York, Washington, D.C., and Pennsylvania.
2004 Hurricane Ivan devastates 90 percent of Grenada Island.	**2003** War in Iraq begins.
2005 Hurricane Emily destroys most of Grenada Island.	
2008 Tillman Thomas becomes prime minister.	**2008** The first African-American president of the United States, Barack Obama, is elected.

GLOSSARY

Amerindians
The original people who inhabited the Americas.

animism
The belief that spirits inhabit natural objects such as stones and trees.

colony
A territory that is distant from the country that governs it.

creole
Also called patois, a language that is based on two or more languages.

emancipate
To set free from slavery.

emigrate
To leave one's country and settle in another.

federation
A union of several states.

gross domestic product (GDP)
The total monetary value of goods and services produced in a country in one year.

indentured laborer
A person who is contracted to do manual work for a fixed period of time in exchange for food, shelter, and other necessities.

jab-jab (JAB-jab)
A creole word for "devil".

Lajabless
A devil woman.

lambi (LAM-bi)
Grenadian word for "conch".

obeah
Witchcraft.

petroglyphs
Prehistoric drawings or carvings on rock.

playing mas
Dressing up in costumes and masks during Carnival.

Rastafarianism
A religion that teaches Haile Selassie, a former emperor of Ethiopia, was God and that black people must return to their home, Africa, one day.

saraca (SAH-ra-ca)
Sacrificial feast.

Shango
An African religion with belief in many spirits.

FOR FURTHER INFORMATION

BOOKS

Kilgore, Cindy and Alan Moore. *Adventure Guide Grenada, St. Vincent and the Grenadines.* Edison, NJ: Hunter Publishing, 2007.

Martin, John Angus. *A-Z of Grenada Heritage.* Oxford, England: Macmillan Education, 2007.

WEBSITES

CIA World Factbook: Grenada. https://www.cia.gov/library/publications/theworld-factbook/geos/gj.html

Government of Grenada. www.gov.gd/index.html

Grenada Tourism Information. www.grenadagrenadines.com

How Stuff Works: How Global Warming Works. http://science.howstuffworks.com/global-warming4.htm

Spiceislander.com. www.spiceislander.com/

FILMS

Blinded (2006) is the first full-length feature film to be produced in Grenada. It is about domestic violence; written, produced, and directed by Anderson Quarless.

MUSIC

Grenada Stories and Songs (2009) is a collection of stories told and sung in English and patois, describing Grenadian society, and interspersed with calypso songs sung in French creole or English patois.

BIBLIOGRAPHY

BOOKS

Bendure, Glenda and Friary, Ned. *Eastern Caribbean*. Victoria, Australia: Lonely Planet Publications, 1994.

Crask, Paul. *Grenada, Carriacou, and Petite Martinique*. Bucks, England: Bradt Travel Guides, 2009.

Rogozinski, Jan. *A Brief History of the Caribbean: From the Arawaks and the Caribs to the Present*. Ontario, Canada: Fitzhenry & Whiteside, 2002.

Sinclair, Norma. *Grenada, Isle of Spice*. Oxford, England: Macmillan Education, 2002.

Tramblay, Helene. *A House That Adna Built: A Family in Grenada*. Winnipeg, MB, Canada: Peguis Publications, 1997.

WEBSITES

CIA World Factbook: Grenada. https://www.cia.gov/library/publications/theworld-factbook/geos/gj.html

Government of Grenada. www.gov.gd/index.html

Grenada Tourism Information. www.grenadagrenadines.com

INDEX

INDEX